My Weekly Walk *with God*

Fifty-two Meditations for Prayer Meetings, Church Members, and Small Groups

JANSEN & GLORIA TROTMAN

TEACH Services, Inc.
PUBLISHING
www.TEACHServices.com • (800) 367-1844

World rights reserved. This book or any portion thereof may not be copied or reproduced in any form or manner whatever, except as provided by law, without the written permission of the publisher, except by a reviewer who may quote brief passages in a review.

The author assumes full responsibility for the accuracy of all facts and quotations as cited in this book. The opinions expressed in this book are the author's personal views and interpretations, and do not necessarily reflect those of the publisher.

This book is provided with the understanding that the publisher is not engaged in giving spiritual, legal, medical, or other professional advice. If authoritative advice is needed, the reader should seek the counsel of a competent professional.

All scripture quotations, unless otherwise indicated are taken from the King James Version (KJV). Public Domain

Scripture quotations marked (NKJV) are taken from the New King James Version®. Copyright ©1982 by Thomas Nelson. Used by permission. All rights reserved.

Scripture quotations marked (NIV) are taken from the Holy Bible, New International Version®, NIV®. Copyright © 1973, 1978, 1984, 2011 by Biblica, Inc.™ Used by permission of Zondervan. All rights reserved worldwide. www.zondervan.com The "NIV" and "New International Version" are trademarks registered in the United States Patent and Trademark Office by Biblica, Inc.™

Copyright ©2017 Jansen Trotman and Gloria Trotman
Copyright © 2017 TEACH Services, Inc.
ISBN-13: 978-1-4796-0755-6 (Paperback)
ISBN-13: 978-1-4796-0756-3 (ePub)
ISBN-13: 978-1-4796-0757-0 (Mobi)
Library of Congress Control Number: 2017901258

Published by

www.TEACHServices.com • (800) 367-1844

TABLE OF CONTENTS

A NOTE FROM THE AUTHORS 7
INTRODUCTION: A CALL TO PRAYER 9
    MEDITATION 1   Why Pray? 10
    MEDITATION 2   Daily Prayer: Heaven's Vitamins 12
    MEDITATION 3   Our Great Need 13
    MEDITATION 4   An Unbelievable Promise 15
    MEDITATION 5   Prayer Isn't for Cowards! 17
    MEDITATION 6   God Is Anxious To Say "Yes" 19
    MEDITATION 7   A Call for Intercessors. 21
    MEDITATION 8   Interceding For Family Members. 23
    MEDITATION 9   Interceding For Our Friends 25
    MEDITATION 10   Interceding For Church Leaders 27
    MEDITATION 11   Interceding for Church Members. 29
    MEDITATION 12   Interceding for National Leaders. 31
    MEDITATION 13   Interceding for Missionaries 33
    MEDITATION 14   Praying on Success Mountain. 35
    MEDITATION 15   Praying in the Valley of Despair 37
    MEDITATION 16   A Difficult Prayer to Pray 39
    MEDITATION 17   The Prayer Jesus Refused to Pray 40
    MEDITATION 18   The Hypocrite's Prayer 41
    MEDITATION 19   When Prayer Becomes Sin 42

MEDITATION 20	Faith and Prayer	44
MEDITATION 21	Persevering in Prayer	46
MEDITATION 22	Prayer and Thanksgiving	48
MEDITATION 23	Prayer and Praise	50
MEDITATION 24	The Prayer of Moses	52
MEDITATION 25	Prayer and Forgiveness	54
MEDITATION 26	The Prayer of Jabez	56
MEDITATION 27	The Prayer of Jesus: "Our Father"	58
MEDITATION 28	The Parting Prayer of Jesus	60
MEDITATION 29	The Graveside Prayer of Jesus	62
MEDITATION 30	The Prayer of Jesus for Deliverance	64
MEDITATION 31	Desperate Prayers	66
MEDITATION 32	The Sinner's Prayer	68
MEDITATION 33	Prayer for Healing	70
MEDITATION 34	Praying in Your Storms	72
MEDITATION 35	Praying for the Holy Spirit	74
MEDITATION 36	A Prayer for Understanding of God's Word	76
MEDITATION 37	The Holy Spirit and Prayer	78
MEDITATION 38	Greet Each Morning with Prayer	80
MEDITATION 39	The Overcomer's Prayer	82
MEDITATION 40	Jesus' Prayer for God to Keep Us	84
MEDITATION 41	Prayer for Cleansing	86
MEDITATION 42	Prayer for Unity	88
MEDITATION 43	The Prayer of Penitence	90

MEDITATION 44	"If My People Pray"	92
MEDITATION 45	Waiting on God	94
MEDITATION 46	A Prayer of the Elderly	96
MEDITATION 47	A Young Person's Prayer	98
MEDITATION 48	The Soul Winner's Prayer	100
MEDITATION 49	A Drowning Man's Prayer	102
MEDITATION 50	The Efficacy of Faith	104
MEDITATION 51	Listening to God's Voice	106
MEDITATION 52	The Last Prayer in the Bible	108

A Note from the Authors

We are excited to offer these fifty-two meditations to be used by churches at the weekly prayer meetings, small groups, and by church members. The purpose of this series is to aid in revitalizing the weekly prayer meetings and the prayer lives of church members.

Sometimes our prayers may become routine or "vain repetitions" (Matthew 6:7). There ought to be, instead, a freshness and ever-widening scope in our prayers. The Bible is replete with ideas for our consideration when we talk with our Creator.

These devotionals will help those who lead out in our prayer meetings to have handy thoughts to present and pray about. Members may also be encouraged to study the topics at home prior to the service and come with additional thoughts of their own to share.

My Weekly Walk with God: 52 Meditations for Prayer Meetings, Church Members and Small Groups is a handy tool with readings and discussion questions that will promote lively interaction. Try this new approach to worship and enjoy the blessings that will follow.

What Can We Do To Revive Our Prayer Meetings?

We urge you to make a resolution to brighten the hues in the garden of prayer. Here's how we can do this:

1. Have a meeting of your Prayer Ministries Committee and commit to rebuilding the interest in the prayer service.

2. Prepare and distribute colorful invitations to the church for prayer meetings.

3. Prepare a roster (in consultation with the pastor) of prayer meeting speakers/leaders.

4. Start on time and end on time. Meetings that do not exceed one hour will encourage the church to attend.

5. Be sure to address the needs of church members during the prayer sessions at the weekly prayer meetings.

6. Remember to have activities, music etc. to include and interest the children in the service.

7. Give out prayer request cards each Sabbath before the weekly prayer meeting. These requests will be presented to God at prayer meetings.

8. Pray for the revival of interest in the midweek prayer service.

9. Keep praying for sustained interest in the prayer meetings.

10. Add the prayer meeting to your personal prayer list.

INTRODUCTION
A Call to Prayer

"And call upon me in the day of trouble: I will deliver thee, and thou shalt glorify me" (Ps. 50:15).

"In the day of my trouble I will call upon thee: for thou wilt answer me" (Ps. 86:7).

If ever there was a time when prayer is a necessity, it is now. Global calamities, global economic crises, global epidemics, global social ills, have become commonplace in our era.

*"Troublesome times are here
Filling men's hearts with fear."*

So many factors—personal and national—make prayer of vital importance. We are unable to bear our burdens alone. Not every prayer of ours has been answered the way we desired, but so many have been answered, that it makes us keep on praying. Sometimes, when attempting to pick a rose, we have been pricked by its thorns; but we still continue picking and smelling the roses! There have been times when we have gone strolling on a sunshiny day, but got caught in a chilling downpour of rain; yet, we still go out strolling another day.

Praying may not always get us all we want, but it will always get us all we need. We have discovered that denied requests have often been among our best blessings. We have learned that the real purpose of prayer is not to try to bring God in harmony with us, but to bring us in harmony with Him.

It is more important to be on God's side than to get God to come over to our side. This was the difficult lesson that King Ahab learned (1 Kings 22). In Ahab's determination to get King Jehoshaphat to join him in battle against Ramothgilead, he secured 400 lying prophets to support what he wanted. The one true prophet, Micaiah, Ahab had put in prison. However, Ahab's army was defeated and he died in battle.

Trust God to do always what is best for us. He will never fail you.

MEDITATION 1
Why Pray?

"Pray without ceasing" (1 Thess. 5:17).

Prayer is not an empty soliloquy. We are not talking to ourselves. We are not talking to an invisible One in the sky. We are conversing with a real Person. But more than that, we are conversing with the most important Person in the universe (Ps. 95:3; 135:5; 86:8; Deut. 10:17).

These are days of automated answering services. You dial a telephone number. Then, as soon as the voice at the other end of the line responds, you begin to talk. But wait. After a few seconds you realize that you are talking to a machine. Sometimes we are amused; at other times we get angry or frustrated. Sometimes, after we choose the option to "wait for the next available agent," the wait seems painfully endless and frustrating before a live agent connects with us.

God, however, is constantly on the line. His line is never busy. There is no call waiting. In fact, our Father is standing beside heaven's receiver, ready to answer and help. "And it shall come to pass, that before they call, I will answer; and while they are yet speaking, I will hear" (Isa. 65:24). "The Lord is nigh unto all them that call upon him, to all that call upon him in truth" (Ps. 145:18).

We pray because our loving, heavenly Father loves to converse with us. If we have the time and voice to talk, He is ready to listen. (Ps. 34:15; 1 Peter 3:12; Isa. 1:18; Jer. 33:3, 29:12). He longs for a father-child relationship with us. Jesus taught us to relate to God as "our Father." (Matt. 6:9, 5:16, 45, 23:9; Mark 11:25; Luke 11:13).

We pray because God has rich blessings to bestow on us. (Ps. 81:10; Eph. 1:3; Ps. 68:19; Deut. 28:2; Ps. 21:1–4 NKJV; Prov. 10:6). Who does not like to claim God's blessings?

We pray because it is our lifeline connection to God, the Source of all life. Our strength is renewed. (John 6:35, 48, 10:10). In these days of emotional and physical drainage, we crave seasons of renewal and refreshing.

We pray because it is our armor against the forces of darkness. (1 Peter 5:8; Luke 22:31, 32; Matt. 26:53). No one who cares about life and safety will refuse an opportunity of protection of armor. We all need to be on our guard against dangerous or fatal attacks. Our armor is essential.

We pray because it is our unsurpassed privilege! What better privilege can one ask for? To the man or woman of prayer, the gates of heaven are opened wide, and God's child can walk right into the throne room of the Monarch of the universe.

"Let us therefore come boldly unto the throne of grace, that we may obtain mercy, and find grace to help in time of need" (Heb. 4:16).

DISCUSSION TIME

1. What should be our motives for prayer? List at least four.

2. How does access to our heavenly Father differ from telephone access to an earthly agent?

3. What benefits can we get from approaching the throne boldly?

MEDITATION 2
Daily Prayer: Heaven's Vitamins

"Now when Daniel knew that the writing was signed, he went into his house; and his windows being open in his chamber toward Jerusalem, he kneeled upon his knees three times a day, and prayed, and gave thanks before his God, as he did aforetime" (Dan. 6:10).

There are many advertisements for daily multi-vitamins intended for us to maintain optimum health. Spiritual health is maintained by daily communion with God. "Every day will I bless thee; and I will praise thy name for ever and ever" (Ps. 145:2). "No man high or low…can steadily maintain before his fellow men, a pure, forceful life, unless his life is hid with Christ in God" (White, *Testimonies Vol. 7,* 194). The psalmist found it necessary to pray seven times a day. (Ps. 119:164.) Daniel determined to talk with God three times a day. (Dan. 6:10).

All of the outstanding men and women of God considered daily prayer as necessary as food. They could not live without it. The more time one spends with God, the more enriched his or her life becomes. Great Christian men and women lament that there is not enough time for prayer; some who spent several hours a day in prayer wished it could be more.

Martin Luther declared, "To be a Christian without prayer is no more possible than to be alive without breathing." Ellen White stated that, "Prayer is the breath of the soul. It is the secret of spiritual power. No other means of grace can be substituted and the health of the soul be preserved" (*Gospel Workers,* p. 254*).*

DISCUSSION TIME

1. A bottle of vitamins usually states the nutritional value of its contents. Make a list of the spiritual benefits of daily prayer:

2. See how long you can hold your breath. How did that feel? What are the potential dangers of going without spiritual oxygen?

3. Try praying or praising God seven times a day as the psalmist did. How did that make you feel? Make an effort to keep up this habit.

MEDITATION 3
Our Great Need

"He will regard the prayer of the destitute, and not despise their prayer" (Ps. 102:17).

"And all things, whatsoever ye shall ask in prayer, believing, ye shall receive" (Matt. 21:22).

I had an event to attend. However, my wrinkled shirt needed to be pressed. I turned on the iron and several minutes after that, there was still no heat. I turned the knob one way, then another. There was no light and no heat. I thought, *how could this iron die when it is only a few months old?* I resigned myself to the fact that the iron was not good for anything but the trash receptacle. I proceeded to wrap the cord around it when I noticed that the cord, while near the outlet, had not been plugged into the outlet. Here I was, frustrated by an iron that was turned on but not plugged in! After plugging in the iron, there was power and there was heat.

So often we function without power in our lives, and wonder why. At such times, we need to examine our connection. Samson was designated by God to be the deliverer of his people, Israel, from the domination of the Philistines. But this physically strong man became spiritually and physically crippled when he cut his connection with God. "And she said, The Philistines be upon thee, Samson. And he awoke out of his sleep, and said, I will go out as at other times before, and shake myself. And he wist not that the LORD was departed from him" (Judges 16:20).

A true Christian will maintain his connection with God through daily prayer. (Luke 18:1; Eph. 6:18; 1 Thess. 3:10; Ps. 86:3; 88:9; Matt. 6:11). As the flow of electricity can be blocked or reduced because of some defect in the power cord, so it is with prayer. The flow of power from on high can be blocked in a variety of ways. Sin may be a blocker. Busyness may be a blocker. An unforgiving attitude may be a blocker. Selfishness may be a blocker. Faithlessness may be a blocker.

Let us examine our prayer life and see if there are any defects in the power cord, and remove them with the help of the Holy Spirit.

DISCUSSION TIME

1. List your three greatest needs in order of importance.

2. What are some "blockers" to our connection with God?

3. Write a prayer to help you keep your connection with God.

4. How can we tell when we are losing our connection with God?

MEDITATION 4
An Unbelievable Promise

"And whatsoever ye shall ask in my name, that will I do, that the Father may be glorified in the Son. If ye shall ask any thing in my name, I will do it" (John 14:13, 14).

"And in that day ye shall ask me nothing. Verily, verily, I say unto you, whatsoever ye shall ask the Father in my name, he will give it you" (John 16:23).

"Hitherto have ye asked nothing in my name: ask, and ye shall receive, that your joy may be full" John 16:24.

Imagine your delight if you had a billionaire friend who gave you a blank check and told you that you could cash it for any amount you wanted to! Would you refuse it? Would you put it away in a cabinet drawer and forget about it? Would you continue to flounder in your little world of debt and financial deprivation? What would you do with it?

We have more than a blank check from a billionaire. Our check is from the richest Person in the universe! "The earth is the Lord's, and the fullness thereof; the world, and they that dwell therein" (Ps. 24:1). "'The silver is mine, and the gold is mine,' saith the Lord of hosts" (Hag. 2:8). Pull up a chair. Sit down with your heavenly Father and ask. He will give you "the desires of your heart" (Ps. 37:4 NKJV). When God finds persons He can trust with unlimited power, He will give them unlimited power.

God, in His wisdom, and for our safety, sometimes withholds some of our desires from us. There are enough examples in Scripture that show us how something that we perceive may be good for us, may actually be bad for us! Israel's request for a king was not good for them. Hezekiah's request for extended life turned out to be a mistake. While we may ask for anything, we must trust God to give us only what is best for us. "No good thing will He withhold from them that walk uprightly" (Ps. 84:11).

He is too wise to give us something that is not best for us. He is too loving to give us something that is not good. We need to realize that in times when we do not understand God's plan, we could still trust His leading. Whatever God allows to come your way has a benefit wrapped inside.

That is why Job, in the midst of his suffering, could exclaim, "Though He slay me, yet will I trust in Him" (Job 13:15).

DISCUSSION TIME

1. Can you think of a promise made to you, which was recently broken? How did that make you feel?

2. Think of three promises you would like to make to God today. Write them down.

3. There have been prayer requests in your life that God withheld from you. Why do you think this happened? Have you been able to see the benefits?

4. What explanation would you give to a friend who is crushed because his/her prayer was not answered?

MEDITATION 5
Prayer Isn't for Cowards!

"So let's walk right up to him and get what he is so ready to give. Take the mercy, accept the help" (Heb. 4:16, MSG).

God is looking for some brave warriors who dare to take Him at His word. One day when Jesus was in Capernaum, a centurion came to Him with a request for his servant's healing. "But speak the word only, and my servant shall be healed." Jesus marveled at these words of belief, faith and trust. "Go thy way; and as thou hast believed, so be it done unto thee. And his servant was healed in the selfsame hour" (Matt. 8:8, 13).

God is looking for radical faith; for a person who will trust Him so completely that he is willing to risk everything to do what Jesus says or wants. Note the powerful words of commitment spoken by Paul, the apostle in Philippians 3:

But what things were gain to me, those I counted loss for Christ. Yea doubtless, and I count all things but loss for the excellency of the knowledge of Christ Jesus my Lord: for whom I have suffered the loss of all things, and do count them but dung, that I may win Christ, and be found in him, not having mine own righteousness, which is of the law, but that which is through the faith of Christ, the righteousness which is of God by faith: that I may know him, and the power of his resurrection, and the fellowship of his sufferings, being made conformable unto his death. (Philippians 3:7–10)

Are you ready to march to the drum beat of heaven? It was Henry David Thoreau, in his literary work, *Walden,* who said these immortal words, "If a man does not keep pace with his companions, perhaps it is because he hears a different drummer. Let him step to the music which he hears, however measured or far away." [1] We admire men like Moses, who, at God's command, marched into the palace of Pharaoh and demanded for God, "Let my people go." Only a few months before, Moses was a reluctant messenger when God recruited him. (Exodus chapters 3, 4, 5). But faith increases when it is exercised. So with holy boldness, Moses fearlessly confronted the pompous, heathen monarch.

---

1. Henry David Thoreau, *Walden,* chapter 18, p. 430 (1966). Originally published in 1854.

We admire men like Joshua, who could dare to ask the impossible that the sun should stand still. When we realize that the sun moves with the entire solar system, and the solar system moves within the framework of the entire Milky Way galaxy, we see what a daring request that was! But God honored it and the sun stood still.

Come boldly to the throne with your request.

DISCUSSION TIME

1. Share with someone the example of boldness that Moses and Joshua showed in today's lesson. When was the last time you exhibited boldness? What was the result?

2. Why do we say that prayer is not for cowards? What are some "risky" prayers that you have offered?

3. What biblical encouragement do we have to make us bold in our prayers?

MEDITATION 6
God Is Anxious To Say "Yes"

"Then shalt thou call, and the LORD shall answer; thou shalt cry, and he shall say, Here I am" (Isa. 58:9).

"And it shall come to pass, that before they call, I will answer; and while they are yet speaking, I will hear" (Isa. 65:24).

Nothing can be more frustrating to a child than to be turned down when he or she makes a legitimate request. Sometimes a parent may be limited in the resources or ability and is therefore unable to grant the request. As a parent, I can understand this limitation. We may approach a lending institution for money to purchase a house or a car or to get funding for education; but our application may be denied because our credit score is not satisfactory.

When we approach the bank of heaven, the One in charge is anxious to say, "Yes." Often our only drawback is our lack of faith. "But without faith it is impossible to please him: for he that cometh to God must believe that he is, and that he is a rewarder of them that diligently seek him" (Heb. 11:6). At times, it may be our bad spiritual credit. "He that turneth away his ear from hearing the law, even his prayer shall be abomination" (Prov. 28:9). "If I regard iniquity in my heart, the Lord will not hear me" (Ps. 66:18). It was Eliphaz the Temanite who reminded Job:

Which doeth great things and unsearchable; marvelous things without number: who giveth rain upon the earth, and sendeth waters upon the fields: to set up on high those that be low; that those which mourn may be exalted to safety. He disappointeth the devices of the crafty, so that their hands cannot perform their enterprise. (Job 5:9–12)

So often I have received a blessing from God that I did not even ask for. God says, "Before they call, I will answer; and while they are yet speaking, I will hear" (Isa. 65:24). What an assurance this is! I remember times when God provided for me during my days in college. On more than one occasion, when I needed money for my college tuition, before I prayed for help, God impressed someone to send me just the amount I needed. Our heavenly Father truly cares for us and is anxious to say, "Yes" to our requests. We can cast all our cares upon Him. (1 Peter 5:7). We must cast all of our cares, not some of our cares on Him. God is inviting us, "Give it all to Me. I can handle it all."

DISCUSSION TIME

1. Share an experience when God provided for you just on time.

2. Share an experience when God provided for you way in advance. How did that make you feel?

3. Have you sometimes worried so much that you almost got sick? How did God come through for you?

4. Write a song/poem or psalm that talks about God as your Provider.

MEDITATION 7
A Call for Intercessors

"And he saw that there was no man, and wondered that there was no intercessor: therefore his arm brought salvation unto him; and his righteousness, it sustained him" (Isa. 59:16).

"No one prays aright who seeks a blessing for himself alone" (White, Thoughts from the Mount of Blessing, 105).

Heaven will be filled with people who got there because someone prayed for them. There will be children who are there because their godly parents persisted in prayer on their behalf. There will be spouses whose partners prayed for their salvation for many years. From all walks of life, there will be those who found the Savior, Jesus, because someone prayed for them. This is the power of intercessory prayer.

All of us need to have a burden on our hearts to intercede for someone. We must feel the passion for the salvation of someone. There may be a man, woman, young person or child, who may not even be interested in his or her own salvation. However, we must intercede for them. It is the intercessor who stands between the wrath of God and the transgressor.

Moses was an unparalleled intercessor. The children of Israel had sinned grievously by making and worshipping the golden calf. This took place right after the Sinai experience. God was ready to destroy the blatant sinners. At this time, Moses intervened and pleaded with God to spare the lives of the people. God responded positively and the people were saved from annihilation! (Exod. 32:30–34).

Miriam and Aaron, the siblings of Moses spoke against him. Miriam criticized Moses for marrying a Cushite woman. Together, Miriam and Aaron talked against Moses, their leader. "And they said, Hath the LORD indeed spoken only by Moses? hath he not spoken also by us? And the LORD heard it" (Num. 12:2). "And the anger of the LORD was kindled against them …" (Num. 12:9). God was ready to punish them. Miriam became a leper. At this point, Moses interceded with God and Miriam was healed—the power of intercessory prayer!

Only God knows how many persons will be saved in His kingdom through our intercessory prayers. There are persons we can intercede for regularly. It is not good enough to limit our prayers to our personal wish list. We must include others: world leaders, church leaders, those incarcerated, victims of addiction, service men and women. As an intercessor, you are a partner with the supreme Intercessor—the Lord Jesus Christ.

DISCUSSION TIME

1. Why do you think it is important to be an intercessor? Can you name some intercessors in the Bible?

2. Make a list of persons for whom you could intercede regularly. Do not just intercede for persons you like: family, or your acquaintances. Include world leaders, church leaders, the homeless, those incarcerated, victims of addiction and domestic violence, service men and women, refugees, etc.

3. Have you sometimes heard the voice of God impressing you to intercede for someone? Could you share this experience?

MEDITATION 8
Interceding For Family Members

There was a man in the land of Uz, whose name was Job; and that man was perfect and upright, and one that feared God, and eschewed evil. And there were born unto him seven sons and three daughters. ... And his sons went and feasted in their houses, every one his day; and sent and called for their three sisters to eat and to drink with them. And it was so, when the days of their feasting were gone about, that Job sent and sanctified them, and rose up early in the morning, and offered burnt offerings according to the number of them all: for Job said, It may be that my sons have sinned and cursed God in their hearts. Thus did Job continually. (Job 1:1, 2, 4, 5)

Job consistently praying for his family members is exemplary. No wonder God held him in such high regard. Job was not sure what his children might have been doing; but he felt sure that his prayers could unleash God's protection for them. By fervent prayer, we can make a hedge about our children.

We need to pray because we would like our children to be happy and successful. This is not only because it makes them enjoy a productive life; but also because the success or failure of our children impacts our own happiness as parents. The wise man, Solomon, refers to the effects of wayward and wise children, on their parents. "A foolish son is the calamity of his father" (Prov. 19:13). "My son, if thine heart be wise, my heart shall rejoice, even mine" (Prov. 23:15).

Even if family members are unlovable, that does not relieve us of our obligation to pray for them. In fact, those who frustrate us the most are in greater need of our prayers. Jesus knew the character of Judas. He knew that Judas was an evil person; yet He kept him close to Himself. Jesus was challenged by the selfish, brooding spirit of Judas, day after day; but He treated him with love as a lesson to His other disciples. (White, *Education*, p. 91–93). Let our love motivate us to intercede for our family members.

Sometimes our children may be like the prodigal that Jesus talked about in Luke 15. They may be in the far country of sin and wretchedness, wasting their lives in ungodly things; but the fervent prayers of Christian parents and relatives will often bring them back to their godly roots. Never give up praying for them. For God sees every tear you shed, and hears every prayer you utter. Then, when you least expect it, you may see the returning prodigal coming home. Just keep on praying until light breaks through.

DISCUSSION TIME

1. Why do you think we ought to pray for our family members?

2. Take some time to list the needs of each family member. Look at photos of them to help you remember them. Make a prayer schedule for them. Check off the prayers that have been answered for them.

3. Look around the church and community and 'adopt' extended family members you would like to pray for.

4. Go for a walk in your neighborhood. As you pass the houses, say a prayer for the persons in those homes.

MEDITATION 9
Interceding For Our Friends

"And the LORD restored Job's losses when he prayed for his friends. Indeed the LORD gave Job twice as much as he had before" (Job 42:10 NKJV).

It is inconceivable that one would call another his or her friend and withhold the best free gift from that friend. The gift of our prayers is free! We do not have to purchase it. Not only is it free, but it is a gift that we can give over and over again. Day after day, we can cover our friends with our prayers. That is what Job did. Interceding for his friends came naturally to him. Even when Job's friends were uncomplimentary, he still prayed for them.

Praying for others has a twofold benefit. It releases God's blessings on our friends. It also releases God's blessings on us (Job 42:10). The Lord restored the fortunes of Job when he prayed for his friends.

There are different opportunities that are presented for praying for our friends:

The prompting of the Holy Spirit. Sometimes we have a continuous urge to pray for a friend. It is an inescapable command. We are not satisfied until we have prayed for that person.

Scheduled prayer sessions for them. We could decide on special times to pray for our friends. It is a good idea to shoot arrow prayers for them even outside of our scheduled time. It is praying without ceasing.

Prayer requests. Sometimes one may say to us, "Please pray for me." That is an opportunity to pray for that person. It is an invitation to pray for them. We may even pray right then and there.

Spontaneous praying for your friends. Have you ever felt that you wanted to pray for a friend? You found yourself praying several times that day for him/her. Then you later discovered that your friend had been in trouble at that same time you felt impressed to pray.

A prayer log. Make a list of your friends, their challenges, their goals. From time to time, pick up the log and pray over it.

Birthdays/anniversaries/ other special days. Pray for our friends on their special occasions.

Praying reacts on the *pray-er* in positive ways. Sincere praying draws us closer to God and the closer one gets to God, the better a person he or she becomes; and the better people become, the more blessings they attract. Many persons have been saved from trouble because there was someone who prayed for them. You may never know what heavenly power was released to help a friend in need, until on the streets of gold it will be revealed to you. Legions of powerful, holy angels have been dispatched in answer to prayer, to deliver one who was in grave danger. This was the case when Peter was in prison awaiting execution. God answered in a dramatic fashion (Acts 12).

DISCUSSION TIME

1. What are two of the benefits of praying for our friends?

2. What are some opportunities we have to pray for our friends?

3. What are some blessings that we may lose by not praying for our friends?

4. Can you think of any biblical examples, apart from Job, where there was intercession for friends?

MEDITATION 10
Interceding For Church Leaders

"Praying always with all prayer and supplication in the Spirit, and watching thereunto with all perseverance and supplication for all saints; and for me, that utterance may be given unto me, that I may open my mouth boldly, to make known the mystery of the gospel" (Eph. 6:18, 19)

"Now I beseech you, brethren, for the Lord *Jesus Christ's sake, and for the love of the Spirit, that ye strive together with me in your prayers to God for me"* (Rom. 15:30).

If there is one category of persons that needs more prayer than others, it is those who are God's ministers. A.W. Tozer, a master preacher, and author, of the 20th century, remarks that ministers are Satan's special targets. There is no other group that he hates more viciously.

If Satan can destroy those who are the leaders in the church of God, it would unsettle the congregation. "Smite the shepherd, and the sheep of the flock shall be scattered abroad" (Matt. 26:31). Behind the masks that many church leaders wear, are burdened, struggling souls who need the prayers of those they serve.

The great apostle, Paul, repeatedly requested the prayers of the believers on his behalf. By praying for our leaders, we build a hedge of protection around them. By our prayers, our leaders also are bestowed with wisdom from heaven. They need this wisdom to help them in making critical decisions. Our prayers also place them in the holy presence of God and His angels. Our prayers cement church leaders' connection with heaven. When we pray for the leaders of the church, our hearts are touched with compassion and understanding for them. We are prone to be less critical and instead enter into an emotional partnership with them for the work of the Lord.

So, let's pray for the church leaders. "Our prayers need most to be offered for the men in high places" (White, *Christian Service*, 148).

DISCUSSION TIME

1. How can praying for our church leaders benefit them? How can it benefit us?

2. Should we still pray for leaders who seem unworthy? Why?

3. How should we relate to our leaders who keep making mistakes?

4. Write a prayer for your leaders.

MEDITATION 11
Interceding for Church Members

"Confess your faults one to another, and pray one for another, that ye may be healed. The effectual fervent prayer of a righteous man availeth much" (James 5:16)

I need the prayers of those I love,
While traveling o'er life's rugged way;
To bear my tempted soul above
That God would help me every day.
(James D. Vaughn, Public Domain)

These lines express the concern of all Christians. So often we are buffeted and tried by the assaults of the enemy and by the vicissitudes of life, that we need the strength that comes from the prayers of our brothers and sisters. One of my most touching experiences was when one of my church members told me, "Pastor, you are always in my prayers." I felt as if a vessel of joy was broken and streams of joy flowed throughout my being. The awareness of sincere persons lifting you up in prayer, gives uncommon strength.

Imagine how Peter must have felt when he was facing his test. The urge to deny his Lord was overpowering. Peter actually succumbed to it. He denied Jesus. Soon after that, feelings of guilt and remorse overcame Peter. Just then, he recalled the loving words that Jesus had spoken to him recently: "Simon, Simon, behold, Satan hath desired to have you, that he may sift you as wheat: but I have prayed for thee, that thy faith fail not: and when thou art converted, strengthen thy brethren" (Luke 22:31–32). "I have prayed for you." What an encouraging, redeeming echo!

When was the last time we told a member of our body of Christ, "I prayed for you?" When was the last time we said to a sister or a brother, "I am praying for you." Try saying these words of solace to someone today. Jesus also prays for each of us:

"Who then is the one who condemns? No one. Christ Jesus who died—more than that, who was raised to life—is at the right hand of God and is also interceding for us" (Rom. 8:34 NIV).

"Therefore he is able to save completely those who come to God through him, because he always lives to intercede for them" (Heb. 7:25 NIV).

Let us also pray for one another.

DISCUSSION TIME

1. What would you give as the most important reason for our interceding for our brothers and sisters?

2. How does our interceding help our brothers and sisters?

3. What are some circumstances that could lead us to intercede for our brothers and sisters?

4. Can you recall a time when someone interceded for you?

MEDITATION 12
Interceding for National Leaders

"I exhort therefore, that, first of all, supplications, prayers, intercessions, and giving of thanks, be made for all men; for kings, and for all that are in authority; that we may lead a quiet and peaceable life in all godliness and honesty. For this is good and acceptable in the sight of God our Saviour; Who will have all men to be saved, and to come unto the knowledge of the truth" (1 Tim. 2:1–4).

The leaders of the countries and nations hold their positions by God's allowance. "Let every soul be subject unto the higher powers. For there is no power but of God: the powers that be are ordained of God" (Rom. 13:1).

God sets up and removes national leaders. "And he changeth the times and the seasons: he removeth kings, and setteth up kings: he giveth wisdom unto the wise, and knowledge to them that know understanding" (Dan. 2:21).

Note the dramatic control God took of King Nebuchadnezzar in his display of pride:

The king spake, and said, Is not this great Babylon, that I have built for the house of the kingdom by the might of my power, and for the honour of my majesty? While the word was in the king's mouth, there fell a voice from heaven, saying, O king Nebuchadnezzar, to thee it is spoken; the kingdom is departed from thee. And they shall drive thee from men, and thy dwelling shall be with the beasts of the field: they shall make thee to eat grass as oxen, and seven times shall pass over thee, until thou know that the most High ruleth in the kingdom of men, and giveth it to whomsoever he will. The same hour was the thing fulfilled upon Nebuchadnezzar: and he was driven from men, and did eat grass as oxen, and his body was wet with the dew of heaven, till his hairs were grown like eagles' feathers, and his nails like birds' claws. And at the end of the days I Nebuchadnezzar lifted up mine eyes unto heaven, and mine understanding returned unto me, and I blessed the most High, and I praised and honoured him that liveth for ever, whose dominion is an everlasting dominion, and his kingdom is from generation to generation. (Dan. 4:30–34)

So while our leaders govern, it is our responsibility to pray for them, that they will rule according to God's purpose and that they will fulfill His will. Even when we do not understand why certain persons are in power; or when we do not appreciate their leadership, we should still pray for them. I am confident that Nebuchadnezzar converted to the God of heaven, not only because of his punishment, but more so because of Daniel's prayers.

King Solomon could admit "The king's heart is in the hand of the Lord, as the rivers of water: he turneth it withersoever he will" (Prov. 21:1). When Christians pray for national leaders, the King of kings can sway the decisions of leaders and legislators.

DISCUSSION TIME

1. Relate the steps that led to the disgraceful state of Nebuchadnezzar. Point out the role pride played in this.

2. Describe the steps that led to Nebuchadnezzar's restoration.

3. Paraphrase Proverbs 22:1.

4. Do you think we ought to pray for leaders who are ungodly? Give reasons for your answer.

MEDITATION 13
Interceding for Missionaries

"Peter therefore was kept in prison: but prayer was made without ceasing of the church unto God for him" (Acts 12:5).

"And when they had ordained them elders in every church, and had prayed with fasting, they commended them to the Lord, on whom they believed" (Acts 14:23).

"Ye also helping together by prayer for us, that for the gift bestowed upon us by the means of many persons thanks may be given by many on our behalf" (2 Cor. 1:11).

"Brethren, pray for us" (1 Thess. 5:25).

"Finally, brethren, pray for us, that the word of the Lord may have free course, and be glorified, even as it is with you" (2 Thess. 3:1).

Only eternity will reveal the hardships and sufferings some missionaries endured to carry the torch of the gospel to some parts of the world. Our prayers are most needed to sustain these men and women who serve. There are many stories of miraculous interventions and deliverance that these missionaries experienced as a result of the prayers of the saints at the home front.

Peter was kept in prison, awaiting trial and possible execution. The church stormed the gates of heaven with their prayers, and his chains fell off. An angel guided him to freedom. (Acts 12:5–17).

A modern day missionary family was marked for execution because they preached the Word of God in a pagan society. The night when the soldiers came to assassinate them and burn their home, they found the missionaries' home surrounded and fully protected by angelic soldiers. This was the result of prayer! The heathen soldiers had no option but to flee in retreat, leaving the missionary family unharmed. After that incident, many residents of that community became converted!

DISCUSSION TIME

1. Recount some of the difficulties missionaries in the Bible encountered.

2. How can our prayers for missionaries be of benefit to them?

3. Share some experiences you know of modern missionaries.

MEDITATION 14
Praying on Success Mountain

Yours, O LORD, is the greatness, the power and the glory, the victory and the majesty; for all that is in heaven and in earth is Yours; Yours is the kingdom, O LORD, and You are exalted as head over all. Both riches and honor come from You, and You reign over all. In Your hand is power and might; in Your hand it is to make great and to give strength to all. Now therefore, our God, we thank You and praise Your glorious name. But who am I, and who are my people, that we should be able to offer so willingly as this? For all things come from You, and of Your own we have given You. For we are aliens and pilgrims before You, as were all our fathers; our days on earth are as a shadow, and without hope. O LORD our God, all this abundance that we have prepared to build You a house for Your holy name is from Your hand, and is all Your own. (1 Chron. 29:11–16 NKJV).

David surely had it right. All success, honor and riches come from God. We must never be forgetful of this when we reach the top. Consider this admonition of Moses:

"Then you say in your heart, 'My power and the might of my hand have gained me this wealth.' And you shall remember the LORD your God, for it is He who gives you power to get wealth, that He may establish His covenant which He swore to your fathers, as it is this day" (Deut. 8:17, 18).

"Save now, I beseech thee, O Lord: O Lord, I beseech thee, send now prosperity" (Ps. 118:25). King David knew the Source of his success. So did King Solomon also who said, "In the day of prosperity be joyful, but in the day of adversity consider: God also hath set the one over against the other, to the end that man should find nothing after him" (Eccles. 7:14). We need to draw closer to God when we get to the top; for it is so easy to stumble and fall. "No one can stand upon a lofty height without danger" (White, *Education*, 51).

Kings Saul, David, Solomon, and Nebuchadnezzar are all sad examples of successful, powerful persons who allowed their success and promotion to become their downfall. When they were nothing, they were humble servants of God. But when elevation came to them, they forgot the true source of their success. They fell. "For promotion cometh neither from the east, nor from the west, nor from the south. But God is the judge: he putteth down one, and setteth up another" (Ps. 75:6, 7).

David learned the lesson that all of us need to learn. Help and success come not from the hills, but from the Lord. (Ps. 121:1–3, NIV). "Trust ye in the LORD for ever: for in the LORD JEHOVAH is everlasting strength" (Isa. 26:4). When success and promotion come, we must always remember to thank the One who made these possible. It is very easy when we are enjoying the acclaim and plaudits of men, to forget who was behind every step we made. When Nebuchadnezzar forgot, he received a swift lesson from God; and in humility he acknowledged that the Most High God was still in control (Dan. 4:34–37).

When King Herod took the praise for himself, he met with speedy retribution:

"And upon a set day Herod, arrayed in royal apparel, sat upon his throne, and made an oration unto them. And the people gave a shout, saying, It is the voice of a god, and not of a man. And immediately the angel of the LORD smote him, because he gave not God the glory: and he was eaten of worms, and gave up the ghost" (Acts 12:21–23).

If there is a time when we especially need prayer, and when we need to pray, it is in the face of success and when we are enjoying the positions in the high places of honor.

DISCUSSION TIME

1. Describe Nebuchadnezzar's behavior in the midst of his success.

2. How did Herod react to the popularity he experienced?

3. Imagine you have been elevated to a high position. What are some pitfalls you ought to avoid? What should your prayer be?

MEDITATION 15
Praying in the Valley of Despair

*"Yea, though I walk through the valley of the shadow of death, I will fear no evil: for thou art with me; thy rod and thy staff they comfort me. Thou preparest a table before me in the presence of mine enemies: thou anointest my head with oil; my cup runneth over. Surely goodness and mercy shall follow me all the days of my life: and I will dwell in the house of the L*ORD *for ever"* (Ps. 23:4–6).

God not only stands beside us in good times, but also in difficult times. He is not only God of the mountain, but also God of the valley. The God of the day is also the God of the night. During the days of King Ahab, the Syrians attacked Israel, but lost shamefully. Benhadad, the Syrian king claimed that it was because Israel's god was a God of the hills. Therefore, he planned his next attack for the plain or valley. God's prophet assured the king that God would show the Syrians that He was not only God of the hills, but He is also God of the valleys. Israel won another decisive victory:

*"And there came a man of God, and spake unto the king of Israel, and said, Thus saith the L*ORD*, Because the Syrians have said, The L*ORD *is God of the hills, but he is not God of the valleys, therefore will I deliver all this great multitude into thine hand, and ye shall know that I am the L*ORD*. And they pitched one over against the other seven days. And so it was, that in the seventh day the battle was joined: and the children of Israel slew of the Syrians an hundred thousand footmen in one day"* (I Kings 20:28, 29).

Lynda Randle, in her popular song, "God on the Mountain," shares the following lyrics:

Life is easy, when you're up on the mountain
And you've got peace of mind, like you've never known
But things change, when you're down in the valley
Don't lose faith, for you're never alone.
(written by Tracy Dartt)

It is easy to talk of God's goodness when things are going well. But when the music stops and the fanfare dies, many like Elijah, go into the valley of despair. Only a few days before, Elijah had been enjoying his Mount Carmel experience when he had won a stunning victory over the prophets of Baal. Then when it was over, and Jezebel, the wicked queen threatened his life, Elijah sank into despair.

Then Jezebel sent a messenger unto Elijah, saying, So let the gods do to me, and more also, if I make not thy life as the life of one of them by tomorrow about this time. And when he saw that, he arose, and went for his life, and came to Beersheba, which belongeth to Judah, and left his servant there. But he himself went a day's journey into the wilderness, and came and sat down under a juniper tree: and he requested for himself that he might die; and said, It is enough; now, O LORD, take away my life; for I am not better than my fathers (1 Kings 19:2–4).

God quickly reassured the depressed prophet that He was still the Ruler of the world. It is reassuring that the God of the mountain is also the God of the valley.

Sometimes the tornadoes of life leave us feeling devastated. Our dreams turn to nightmares, and our dearest hopes are crushed. We feel helpless and defeated as our goals recede and seem to mock us. Be comforted. God does His best work in the valleys. The Psalmist David was able to reflect, "Yea, though I walk through the valley … thou art with me" (Psalm 23:4).

DISCUSSION TIME

1. Pick one of the mountain top experiences in today's lesson. Discuss it with the group. What do you consider the highlights of this account?

2. Discuss the valley experience of Elijah. What might have caused him to dwell in the valley?

3. What promises in the Bible can comfort us during our valley experiences?

MEDITATION 16
A Difficult Prayer to Pray

"And he went a little farther, and fell on his face, and prayed, saying, O my Father, if it be possible, let this cup pass from me: nevertheless not as I will, but as thou wilt" (Matt. 26:39).

Sometimes our human desires run counter to God's will. This is normal since God's ways are not always our ways; and His thoughts are not always our thoughts. In fact, God's thoughts and ways are vastly different from ours (Isa. 55:8, 9).

Israel agitated for a king because they wanted to be like the surrounding nations. This was contrary to God's will; and He even advised against it. When the nation insisted, God not only cooperated with their request, but He helped in the selection of the king—Saul. Saul turned out to be a disappointment. So did many of the subsequent kings.

It is so much better to trust God's perfect wisdom, instead of our own faulty, selfish desires. We are so often deceived by what is seen. God, however, can see the unseen. He has promised to guide us with His eye. "I will guide thee with mine eye" (Ps. 32:8).

Even Jesus in His humanity demonstrated that the best way to pray is to say, "Thy will be done," even when God's will may lead us through Gethsemane and up to Calvary. It is far better to suffer pain and even death within the will of God, than comfort and extended life outside the will of God.

Knowing that we are walking within the will of God, gives us a courage that conquers fear. "Yea, though I walk through the valley of the shadow of death, I will fear no evil" (Ps. 23:4). God gives us a peace that the world cannot give nor take away.

DISCUSSION TIME

1. What circumstances drove Jesus to ask that, "this cup pass from me?"

2. "Nevertheless, not as I will, but as thou wilt." What is the importance of this part of the prayer of Jesus in the garden before He went to the cross?

3. What should be our attitude when we are tempted to want our will?

4. Can you recall any time when you experienced Psalm 32:8?

MEDITATION 17
The Prayer Jesus Refused to Pray

"I pray not that thou shouldest take them out of the world, but that thou shouldest keep them from the evil" (John 17:15)

Jesus was a Man of prayer. Not only did He believe in prayer; but He taught His disciples the importance of prayer.

Even today, one of the best known passages in the Bible is the Lord's Prayer in Matthew 6:9–13. But there is something that Jesus refused to pray for. He did not just keep silent about it. He mentioned it and said that He would not pray for it. This was His prayer: "I pray not that thou shouldest take them out of the world, but that thou shouldest keep them from the evil" (John 17:15).

Jesus did not want His followers, His disciples, taken out of the world. He knew that the evangelization of this world depended on the loyal followers remaining in the world, so that they could spread the gospel. Earlier in His ministry, Jesus told His disciples, "Ye are the salt of the earth . . . Ye are the light of the world" (Matt. 5:13-14).

Satan has determined to take over Planet Earth, but God has placed an elite fighting force to stop his march and to win the world for Christ. Millions of born again Christians with Bibles in their hands and Jesus in their hearts, are propelled by the Holy Spirit and are going everywhere telling the story of Jesus and His love. The message of a crucified, risen, and soon coming Savior, is being carried through dense jungles, across burning deserts, over mammoth rivers. The message is taken to crowded cities, and sparsely populated islands of the sea.

That's why Jesus did not pray to "take them out of the world." Not yet. But soon the mission will be accomplished, and Jesus will return to take us home.

DISCUSSION TIME

1. What was Jesus' insight in not praying for us to be taken out of this world?

2. Are there some prayers that we should not pray? Give examples.

3. What is the purpose of Jesus' disciples remaining in this world?

4. Discuss the difference between being **in** this world and being **of** this world. What should be the Christian's stance?

MEDITATION 18
The Hypocrite's Prayer

"And when thou prayest, thou shalt not be as the hypocrites are: for they love to pray standing in the synagogues and in the corners of the streets, that they may be seen of men. Verily I say unto you, they have their reward" (Matt. 6:5).

Many public prayers cater to the audience, and are not really conversations with God. God is not concerned with the rhetoric of our prayers—how ornate and flowery they are. He is concerned with how heartfelt and sincere our prayers are. The fact is that we cannot fool God. He knows the genuine from the counterfeit.

Many of us have been deceived by some merchandise we purchased which we believed was real. However, we later discovered that it was truly fake. What a disappointment! No one likes a fraud—a thing or a person. When we come to God, He knows if we are genuine and true. He is annoyed with hypocrites' prayers!

David prayed, "Search me, O God" (Ps. 139:23). We all need that divine help and illumination to help us get real when we come before the God who sees everything. When we come to Him with our broken souls, our loving Savior is ready to mend us. But God cannot fix what we hide from Him. But when we approach Him with all of our broken pieces exposed to Him, Jesus will put them together again and give us a song in our hearts and sincerity in our petitions.

Jesus wants us to be genuine with Him, to put away our masks and costumes, and come to the foot of the cross, and let Him make new persons out of us. "Therefore if any man be in Christ, he is a new creature: old things are passed away; behold, all things are become new" (2 Cor. 5:17).

DISCUSSION TIME

1. What did Jesus notice about the prayer habits of the Pharisees that caused Him to call them hypocrites?

2. What are some possible flaws in our prayers that make us hypocrites?

3. How can we pray so that God will accept our petitions as genuine?

4. Write a prayer to God that you consider heartfelt and sincere.

MEDITATION 19
When Prayer Becomes Sin

"He that turneth away his ear from hearing the law, even his prayer shall be abomination" (Prov. 28:9).

"The sacrifice of the wicked is an abomination to the LORD: but the prayer of the upright is his delight" (Prov. 15:8).

"When he shall be judged, let him be condemned: and let his prayer become sin" (Ps. 109:7).

Prayer and sin do not operate together. Prayer should keep us from sinning, and sin would keep us from praying. When the Pharisees criticized Jesus for healing the blind man (John 9), some of them asked, "How can a man who is a sinner do such miracles?" The healed man challenged the Pharisees, "Now we know that God heareth not sinners: but if any man be a worshipper of God, and doeth his will, him he heareth" (John 9:31).

Prayer becomes sin when it is offered by the willfully disobedient and iniquitous (Prov. 28:9). God will listen to the prayer of the sinner who cries to Him for deliverance from sin. God wants to save from sin not in sin. So God closes His ears to the prayer of one who refuses to give up his sin and turn to God for His mercy and grace.

God will not share the throne of our hearts. The very first of the Ten Commandments states, "Thou shalt have no other gods before me" (Exod. 20:3). For prayer to be effective, it must be offered by one who is prepared to confess and forsake sin.

When we expect important guests, we make sure that our homes are swept and clean. If we expect God to live in our hearts, we must likewise cleanse our hearts with the blood of Christ (James 4:8; 1 John 1:7–9).

DISCUSSION TIME

1. Should we who are sinners attempt to pray to God? Would He not reject our prayers?

2. How can we who are sinners offer prayers to God that He will accept?

3. What does the Bible say about people who persist in their sinful ways? Should they pray at all?

4. What would you say to someone who admits to you his sinful state but wants to pray to God? Is this person hopeless?

MEDITATION 20
Faith and Prayer

"And all things, whatsoever ye shall ask in prayer, believing, ye shall receive" (Matt. 21:22).

Faith is the indispensable companion of prayer. Note the apostle James' declaration: "And the prayer of faith shall save the sick, and the Lord shall raise him up; and if he have committed sins, they shall be forgiven him. Confess your faults one to another, and pray one for another, that ye may be healed. The effectual fervent prayer of a righteous man availeth much" (James 5:15, 16).

The apostle Paul assures us, "But without faith it is impossible to please him: for he that cometh to God must believe that he is, and that he is a rewarder of them that diligently seek him" (Heb. 11:6). One of the beautiful examples of faith in the New Testament, was a Roman centurion:

*And when Jesus was entered into Capernaum, there came unto him a centurion, beseeching him, and saying, L*ORD*, my servant lieth at home sick of the palsy, grievously tormented. And Jesus saith unto him, I will come and heal him. The centurion answered and said, L*ORD*, I am not worthy that thou shouldest come under my roof: but speak the word only, and my servant shall be healed. ...When Jesus heard it, he marveled, and said to them that followed, Verily I say unto you, I have not found so great faith, no, not in Israel. (Matt. 8:5–10)*

The faith of two blind men who came to Jesus for healing, is equally commendable:

*"And when Jesus departed thence, two blind men followed him, crying, and saying, Thou son of David, have mercy on us. And when he was come into the house, the blind men came to him: and Jesus saith unto them, Believe ye that I am able to do this? They said unto him, Yea, L*ORD*. Then touched he their eyes, saying, According to your faith be it unto you" (Matt. 9:27–29).*

The hemorrhaging woman demonstrated remarkable faith when she touched the hem of the garment of Jesus, expecting healing. Jesus acknowledged her faith:

"And he said unto her, Daughter, thy faith hath made thee whole; go in peace, and be whole of thy plague" (Mark 5:34).

As we have seen, one important essential to effective prayer is faith. Faith is believing God so fully that there is no room for doubt. It is acting on what God says, not because it seems logical, reasonable, or politically acceptable, but just because God says so.

Faith manifests itself in the widow, who in time of famine, gave her last meal to the prophet, Elijah, because she believed that God could supply more (1 Kings 17:12–16). Faith is a father bringing his demon-possessed son to Jesus for healing, saying, "Lord, I believe; help thou my unbelief" (Mark 9:24). Faith is a crew of seasoned fishermen who after fishing futilely all night, went out once more to fish at the command of their Lord. These men believed that Jesus knew something they did not know (Luke 5:1–10). This resulted in the largest catch of fish they had ever made!

When we see what God has done for others in the past, it strengthens our own faith in God's ability to solve our problems:

It is no secret what God can do.
What He's done for others, He'll do for you.
With arms wide open, He'll pardon you.
It is no secret what God can do.
Stuart Hamblen

This was Stuart Hamblen's confession of faith when his life was transformed by the power of Jesus.

Read once more the gospels of Matthew, Mark, Luke and John. Reflect on the mighty power resulting from releasing faith in God. Then allow the authenticity of faith in Jesus to generate our own faith in Him.

DISCUSSION TIME

1. What are the essentials for healing?

2. Which of the stories in today's devotional is your favorite and why?

3. Faith is believing God so fully that there is no room for doubt. It is acting on what God says, not because it seems logical, reasonable, or politically acceptable, but just because God says so. Explain.

MEDITATION 21
Persevering in Prayer

*And he spake a parable unto them to this end, that men ought always to pray, and not to faint; saying, There was in a city a judge, which feared not God, neither regarded man: and there was a widow in that city; and she came unto him, saying, Avenge me of mine adversary. And he would not for a while: but afterward he said within himself, Though I fear not God, nor regard man; yet because this widow troubleth me, I will avenge her, lest by her continual coming she weary me. And the L*ORD *said, Hear what the unjust judge saith. (Luke 18:1–6)*

One of the great tragedies of the Christian life is letting go of the Arm of Omnipotence too soon. Sometimes the answer to our prayer is just around the corner, but we turn back because we believe we have walked enough.

Jesus taught that perseverance in prayer is often the key to getting the answer we desire. Prayer is not a vending machine where we put money into a slot, push the select button and out comes the product. Real prayer is conversing with God as our loving, heavenly Father. It is spending time with your best Friend. Therefore, it is not an experience we want to rush through in order to move on to more important business.

By persevering in prayer, we get to learn more about God. We understand Him better. When Moses spent forty days of quality time with God on the mountain, even his outward appearance was transformed (Exod. 34:29–35).

The whole purpose of prayer is not to effect a change in God but to allow God to work a change in us (2 Cor. 3:18). As we persevere in prayer, we learn a lot about ourselves. We do not know ourselves. "The heart is deceitful above all things, and desperately wicked: who can know it?" (Jer. 17:9). God knows us intimately. (Psalm 139:1–6).

If we spend quality time with God, He will show us where we need to develop and grow to become the best we can be, pleasing God day by day.

DISCUSSION TIME

1. "Yet because this widow troubleth me, I will avenge her, lest by her continual coming she weary me." Can we "weary" God? What comparison could we make between God and the unjust judge?

2. What lesson was Jesus trying to teach from this parable?

3. Why should we persevere in prayer? Is it to get an answer or to enrich an experience? Could we still get an answer to our prayer even if we did not persevere? Explain your answer.

MEDITATION 22
Prayer and Thanksgiving

"Be careful for nothing; but in every thing by prayer and supplication with thanksgiving let your requests be made known unto God" (Phil. 4:6).

"Continue in prayer, and watch in the same with thanksgiving" (Col. 4:2).

An old legend tells how God sent two angels from heaven on an assignment. Each angel carried a large basket in which he was to collect the prayers from earth and return to heaven at the end of the day. One angel carried the basket for prayers of thanksgiving; and the other angel's basket was for prayer requests from earth. The angel with the thanksgiving basket returned to heaven in record time. His basket was very light and easy to transport because it was almost empty! But the angel with the request basket was barely able to lift his basket—so heavy and overflowing it was that the angel struggled with its weight. Consequently, he got back to heaven very late.

Legend or not, is this not the way we Christians behave? Do we not spend more of our prayer time making requests than giving thanks to our mighty God? Perhaps it would be well for us to log our requests and compare them with the frequency of our thank you expressions. What a revelation that would be!

What would you think of a father-child relationship in which 90% of the conversation was taken up with the child's requests? Selfish? One-sided? Poor in interaction? On the contrary, picture a different relationship: parent and child exchange ideas, hopes, and dreams. Father is allowed to express love for the child. The child recognizes the parent's love. This child freely verbalizes gratitude and praise for what the parent bestowed. What a heart of thanksgiving is shared!

Requests have their place in our prayers. However, we ought to spend much time giving thanks for the blessings we have already received. What might be helpful, is to keep a log of blessings we received and enjoyed; and count them regularly. As the song says,

Count your blessings,
Name them one by one,

And it will surprise you
What the L<small>ORD</small> *has done!*
Johnson Oatman, Jr. (Public Domain)

Jeremiah points out that God's blessings are new every morning (Lam. 3:21–23). Therefore every day presents new opportunities for thanksgiving. "O give thanks unto the Lord; for he is good" (Ps. 118:1). Today, let us make a choice. Where would our emphasis lie? Requests or praises?

"Bless the L<small>ORD</small>, *O my soul: and all that is within me, bless his holy name. Bless the* L<small>ORD</small>, *O my soul, and forget not all his benefits" (Ps 103:1, 2).*

DISCUSSION TIME

1. "In every thing by prayer and supplication with thanksgiving let your requests be made known unto God" (Phil. 4:6). Think of a request you want to bring to God. Using the formula in Philippians 4:6, write a prayer to God.

2. Make a list of ten benefits you are now enjoying from God.

3. Here is an experiment for you to do at home. Try "blessing the Lord" every hour for the next five hours. How did that make you feel?

MEDITATION 23
Prayer and Praise

"I will bless the LORD at all times: his praise shall continually be in my mouth" (Ps. 34:1)

Praise ye the LORD. Praise God in his sanctuary: praise him in the firmament of his power. Praise him for his mighty acts: praise him according to his excellent greatness. Praise him with the sound of the trumpet: praise him with the psaltery and harp. Praise him with the timbrel and dance: praise him with stringed instruments and organs. Praise him upon the loud cymbals: praise him upon the high sounding cymbals. Let every thing that hath breath praise the LORD. Praise ye the LORD. (Ps. 150)

"For great is the LORD, and greatly to be praised: he also is to be feared above all gods" (1 Chron. 16:25).

Jehoshaphat, king of Judah, was facing seemingly impossible odds. A formidable three-fold alliance was poised to invade his territory and Jehoshaphat was terrified. The king of Judah brought out his most powerful weapon—prayer. He knew that his army was outnumbered by the enemy, but he realized that one with God is a majority. Jehoshaphat turned to God. "Our eyes are upon thee," he prayed (2 Chron. 20:12).

God answered promptly. "Ye shall not need to fight in this battle: set yourselves, stand ye still, and see the salvation of the Lord" (2 Chron. 20:17). "Be not afraid nor dismayed by reason of this great multitude; for the battle is not yours, but God's" (2 Chron. 20:15).

With this encouragement King Jehoshaphat went out to face the enemies. He had an unusual strategy. "He appointed singers unto the LORD, and that should praise the beauty of holiness, as they went out before the army, and to say, Praise the LORD; for his mercy endureth for ever" (2 Chron. 20:21).

And when they began to sing and to praise, the LORD set ambushments against the children of Ammon, Moab, and mount Seir, which were come against Judah; and they were smitten. For the children of Ammon and Moab stood up against the inhabitants of mount

Seir, utterly to slay and destroy them: and when they had made an end of the inhabitants of Seir, every one helped to destroy another. And when Judah came toward the watch tower in the wilderness, they looked unto the multitude, and, behold, they were dead bodies fallen to the earth, and none escaped. And when Jehoshaphat and his people came to take away the spoil of them, they found among them in abundance both riches with the dead bodies, and precious jewels, which they stripped off for themselves, more than they could carry away: and they were three days in gathering of the spoil, it was so much. (2 Chron. 20:22–25)

There is a power in praise that many do not realize. The psalmist declares, "I will bless the Lord at all times; his praise shall continually be in my mouth" (Ps. 34:1). David also stated, "Let my mouth be filled with thy praise and with thy honour all the day" (Ps. 71:8). Charles Wesley caught the spirit of the psalmist, "O for a thousand tongues to sing my great Redeemer's praise."

DISCUSSION TIME

1. Form a group and have each person say one of the praises of Psalm 150.

2. Now go around the group again. Add your own praises to the list in Psalm 150.

3. Write a song or poem of praise. Share it with the group and say what experience prompted you to write that song or poem.

MEDITATION 24
The Prayer of Moses

"And he said, 'I beseech thee, show me thy glory'" (Exod. 33:18).

Moses was undoubtedly one of the most outstanding persons of prayer. He kept close to God, especially from that day of his encounter with God at the burning bush (Exod. 3:2). In fact, God selected him for special, intimate conversations (Exod. 33:11).

In his desire to get even closer to God, Moses prayed, "I beseech thee, show me thy glory" (Exod. 33:18). God honored that prayer; and revealed Himself to Moses as He did to no other person. At the completion of that divine encounter which lasted forty days, Moses' face exhibited a glory and radiance that was blinding to onlookers (Exod. 34:29–35).

The prayer of Moses is one we all need to pray. We should all desire to know God more and better. Eliphaz, the friend of Job, was on track when he said, "Acquaint now thyself with him [God], and be at peace: thereby good shall come unto thee" (Job 22:21). The apostle Paul hungered for a deeper knowledge of Christ (Phil. 3:8–11). He was prepared to give up everything else for that privilege.

When we come to know God, as it is our privilege to know Him through Christ, life will never be the same. We will become reborn, transformed and redirected. We will become new creations with new purposes and new motivations.

Therefore, how can we know God better? We can learn of Him through His creation. The Psalmist states, "The heavens declare the glory of God; and the firmament sheweth his handiwork" (Ps. 19:1). All over the natural world, God's glory shines—from the ant to the elephant, from the smallest grain of sand to the myriads of galaxies in the universe, God's name is written.

We can also know Him through the revelation of His Word. Jesus said, "Search the scriptures; ... and they are they which testify of me" (John 5:39). On every page of the holy Word, God's glory shines in transforming power. Many a sinner has been rescued from chains of darkness, by the entrance of God's Word (Ps. 119:130).

We can also come to know God through our personal experiences. In our everyday activities, we may get to see Him if we would just look. "'And ye shall seek me, and find me, when ye shall search for me with all your heart. And I will be found of you,' saith the Lord" (Jer. 29:13, 14).

DISCUSSION TIME

1. How did the glimpse Moses got of the glory of God affect him? What does this tell us about our closeness to God?

2. Has anyone ever looked at you and asked if you were a Christian because they thought you looked like one? What do you think would have prompted a question like that?

3. Make a list of transformations that could take place in us after we have had a glimpse of Jesus.

MEDITATION 25
Prayer and Forgiveness

"And forgive us our debts, as we forgive our debtors. And lead us not into temptation, but deliver us from evil: for thine is the kingdom, and the power, and the glory, for ever. Amen. For if ye forgive men their trespasses, your heavenly Father will also forgive you: but if ye forgive not men their trespasses, neither will your Father forgive your trespasses" (Matt. 6:12–15).

"And when ye stand praying, forgive, if ye have ought against any: that your Father also which is in heaven may forgive you your trespasses" (Mark 11:25).

In His model prayer that Jesus taught His disciples, forgiveness for others was a central element. An unforgiving spirit will certainly block answers to our prayers. God expects us to forgive those who have wronged us, just as freely as He forgives us. Jesus clearly states that it is pointless to ask God to forgive us if we do not forgive others.

When the disciples queried about the nature of forgiveness, Jesus told the parable of two debtors (Matthew 18:23-25). One servant owed the king an exorbitant sum which he could not repay. The king had mercy on him when he pleaded for forgiveness and canceled his debt. Soon after he became debt-free, the forgiven servant met a man who had owed him a small sum of money. He promptly attacked his debtor in a most unsympathetic manner and demanded immediate payment. Word of his unforgiving attitude soon reached the king. The king immediately arrested the unforgiving man and threw him in prison, where he was forced to remain, until the debt he had originally owed the king was paid in full!

Jesus was making it clear that we must forgive others to be forgiven by God. Forgiveness isn't always easy, but it is always godly and right. When Jesus, our Master, was being crucified, He demonstrated this teaching. "Father, forgive them; for they know not what they do" (Luke 23:34). Following in the footsteps of the Master, Stephen, when he was being stoned to death, prayed, "Lay not this sin to their charge" (Acts 7:60). What an example for the rest of us!

DISCUSSION TIME

1. With which of the characters in the story Jesus told do you prefer to identify? Why?

2. Someone is always watching us. Do we realize that people are looking at us and taking note of our unforgiving attitude?

3. What are some things that keep us from forgiving? (Pride? The urge to punish the offender? Other?)

4. God will not hear our prayers if we do not forgive our debtors. What makes us all keep praying to God? Is it that we do not remember that we need to forgive someone? How can we avoid this pitfall?

5. What does it mean to forgive and forget? Can we forgive without forgetting? Share your understanding of this concept.

MEDITATION 26
The Prayer of Jabez

"And Jabez called on the God of Israel, saying, Oh that thou wouldest bless me indeed, and enlarge my coast, and that thine hand might be with me, and that thou wouldest keep me from evil, that it may not grieve me! And God granted him that which he requested" (1 Chron. 4:10).

We don't know much about Jabez, except that he is a descendant of King David. However, his prayer has made him famous. It is a short, but heartfelt prayer with which we all could identify.

Jabez asked God for His blessing. What would life be without God's blessing? When God blesses someone, success and goodwill follow him like a shadow that never leaves him. Abraham is an example of this (Gen. 12:2; 22:17). The blessings of God are contingent on our obedience (Deut. 28:1–2).

Jabez also prayed for enlargement of his territory. God has promised to prosper those who are obedient and faithful to Him. The basis on which God enlarges our territory is our faithfulness in the small tasks He gives us (Matt. 25:21; Luke 16:10). Daniel was promoted from captive to prime minister because of his faithfulness. Joseph was elevated from slave to the second in command in all of Egypt.

Jabez requested God's guidance. The only safe path to follow is the one that God chooses for us. God has promised safe and secure guidance (Ps. 32:8). The condition is submission to His will. "In all thy ways acknowledge him, and he shall direct thy paths" (Prov. 3:6).

Jabez asked God to keep him from evil. God loves to answer that request. Jesus Himself asked His Father to keep His followers from evil in the world (John 17:15). This may be a two-pronged request. We need God to keep us from doing evil, and we need to be preserved from evil being done to us.

The mother of Jabez so named him because of the painful childbirth she experienced with him. Jabez did not want his actions to cause pain to others, so he prayed to be kept from evil deeds.

God granted Jabez's requests. When we honor God by our lives, He, in turn, will honor us (1 Sam. 2:30). It is the law of the harvest. What we sow, we will reap.

DISCUSSION TIME

1. Take a look once more at the prayer of Jabez. Apply each item in the prayer to your life and pray for yourself. For example: Ask God to bless you in a particular area. Think of a territory you would like God to enlarge for you. Ask God to guide you as you pursue specific plans. Continue to pray this prayer for several days and wait to see how God fulfills your requests. Make a note in your journal.

2. Jabez prayed that God would keep him from evil. Think of how our thoughtless, evil ways affect others as well as they affect us. Reflect on how the devil is working to keep us **in** evil. Ask God daily to keep you **from** evil.

3. Read the prayer of Jabez once more. Memorize it. Repeat it often inserting your name and the names of your loved ones.

MEDITATION 27
The Prayer of Jesus: "Our Father"

"After this manner therefore pray ye: Our Father which art in heaven, Hallowed be thy name. Thy kingdom come, Thy will be done in earth, as it is in heaven. Give us this day our daily bread. And forgive us our debts, as we forgive our debtors. And lead us not into temptation, but deliver us from evil: for thine is the kingdom, and the power, and the glory, for ever. Amen. (Matt. 6:9–13).

At the request of the disciples to be taught how to pray, Jesus offered this model. It is the best-known prayer, but few understand the full import of its message.

True prayer begins with a proper understanding of the object of our prayers. In prayer, we are conversing with our heavenly Father. "Father" was Jesus' preferred title for "God." We can think of many majestic and powerful names for God, but "Father" is the most endearing. We can approach Him without fear, knowing that He loves us and has our best interest in mind.

Anyone who has had a loving father understands a little of what God is to us. God is not a cosmic policeman waiting to catch us doing wrong so He can arrest us and punish us. He is not a fearsome, irritable judge who is annoyed when we appear in His courtroom once more.

God is a loving Father who enjoys the company of His children. God is a loving Father who has only good thoughts towards His children. He wants to supply our needs out of His riches in glory by Christ Jesus (Phil. 4:19). He watches over His children with a protecting eye, ready to defend them from danger. We have a compassionate Father who watches by the bedside of His sick child and desires to heal their diseases (Ps. 103:3).

It is a pity that not all earthly fathers reflect the Father who is in heaven. It is comforting to know that at times when earthly parents disappoint and hurt us, we can turn to our Father who is in heaven. We can turn to our Father whose arms are always open to us. He is a father who loves us unconditionally. He cares for us unceasingly. He provides for us generously. He protects us faithfully.

DISCUSSION TIME

1. "Our Father which art in heaven." Many children cannot locate their fathers. Many families have absentee fathers. What are the advantages of knowing where our Father is and of being able to go to Him in time of need?

2. How does our loving heavenly Father differ from some earthly fathers?

3. Create a word picture of an ideal earthly father.

MEDITATION 28
The Parting Prayer of Jesus

"I have glorified thee on the earth: I have finished the work which thou gavest me to do" (John 17:4).

John 17 records the longest recorded prayer of the Savior. He was accustomed to spending entire nights in prayer. This was a different prayer. The shadow of the cross loomed over Him. He knew that He would be paying the ultimate price for man's salvation. "The hour is come" (John 17:1). Jesus' earthly ministry was at an end. "I have finished the work which thou gavest me to do" (John 17:4). Later, the apostle Paul could say of himself as he was nearing death, "I have fought a good fight, I have finished my course" (2 Tim. 4:7). To faithfully complete our mission in life should be our goal.

There is a sense of satisfaction and peace that comes to the servant of God when he or she arrives at the completion of the task God assigned. Each of us has been placed on this earth for a purpose. We ask ourselves the lingering philosophical question, *why am I here*? Each of us needs to find God's purpose for our life and fulfill it. We dare not leave an unfinished task behind!

Jesus knew why He was born. "Pilate therefore said unto him, Art thou a king then? Jesus answered, Thou sayest that I am a king. To this end was I born, and for this cause came I into the world, that I should bear witness unto the truth. Every one that is of the truth heareth my voice" (John 18:37). Jesus knew that he came to give His life as a ransom for many (Matt. 20:28).

So, in this great prayer, Jesus asked His heavenly Father to put His stamp of approval on the work that He had done. "And now, O Father, glorify thou me with thine own self with the glory which I had with thee before the world was" (John 17:5). God has work for everyone to do. A post of responsibility has been assigned to each person in His kingdom. At the end of life's journey, may we be able to say, "I have finished the work which thou gavest me to do."

DISCUSSION TIME

1. What does this prayer of Jesus tell us about how Jesus felt about His mission?

2. The three philosophical questions in life are, *where did I come from, why am I here, where am I going?* Reflect on each of these questions. What answers can you give?

3. We have all had an assignment to complete at some time or another. What type of evaluation makes us happy?

4. What heavenly evaluation are we working for now?

MEDITATION 29
The Graveside Prayer of Jesus

"Then they took away the stone from the place where the dead was laid. And Jesus lifted up his eyes and said, Father, I thank thee that thou hast heard me. And I knew that thou hearest me always; but because of the people which stand by, I said it, that they may believe that thou hast sent me" (John 11:41, 42).

Jesus was a firm believer in God who could do what men thought was impossible (Matt. 19:26; Mark 9:23, 14:36). He faced a doubting crowd at the graveside of Lazarus. *Whoever heard of one who could raise the dead?* Jesus did not honor their unbelief with an answer or an argument. He pursued His purpose. He was not going to be sidetracked. This is an example for us. We may be caught in the midst of scoffing and unbelief, but we must stick to our purpose. We must do the work that God intended for us to do.

Raising the dead was not a challenge because of Jesus' closeness to His heavenly Father. He knew that God the Father always listened to His prayer. So He prayed with confidence in front of the open sepulcher in which Lazarus had been placed four days before.

Even Mary and Martha, His close friends, believed that Jesus could heal the sick, but raising the dead was beyond His ability. Jesus prayed at the graveside to show us that there are no hopeless situations with God. So often we have felt bewildered and impotent before a problem or difficulty, forgetting that our heavenly Father waits for us to ask Him for His help (Matt. 7:7–8, 21:22). No sincere prayer is ever ignored by Him. God knows what we need even before we ask Him. "No good thing will he withhold from them that walk uprightly" (Ps. 84:11).

When we develop the habit of praying always and receiving answers, it becomes easier to exercise our faith, even when we face challenges. Jesus did not wait until He needed a resurrection miracle to discover the power of prayer. He had a track record in prayer. So should we.

DISCUSSION TIME

1. How did Jesus react to the doubting crowd at the tomb of Lazarus? How should we react when others express doubt that God is able?

2. We need to share our testimonies about the ability and power of God to help us. Can you remember a time when God did the "impossible" for you? Did you share this experience?

3. What part does constant prayer play in developing our faith in God?

4. What are some steps we can take to develop a relationship with Jesus?

MEDITATION 30
The Prayer of Jesus for Deliverance

"And he went a little farther, and fell on his face, and prayed, saying, O my Father, if it be possible, let this cup pass from me: nevertheless not as I will, but as thou wilt" (Matt. 26:39).

"The gulf … was so deep, that His spirit shuddered before it" (White, *Desire of Ages,* 686). Jesus was balancing on the brink of the precipice of death. This He was facing not for Himself, but for us. He saw the terrors of eternal separation from God; and wondered if we were worth it (White, *Desire of Ages,* 753). He concluded that if the only way you and I could be saved is through His sacrifice, He would drink the bitter cup of death (Isa. 53). He took our place. Jason Crabb captures the irony:

Who am I that the King would bleed and die for?
*Who am I that He would pray not my will, Thine L*ORD*?*
The answer I may never know,
Why He ever loved me so
But to that old rugged cross He'd go, For who am I?
(Charles "Rusty" Goodman)

There are some situations in life from which we want deliverance. We find ourselves praying as did Jesus, "Let this cup pass from me." It may be a painful terminal illness, from which we see no relief. It may be a wayward spouse or child who seems impervious to all attempts to reach him or her with the gospel. It may be stress on the job, harassment by employers or co-workers. Whatever the bitter cup we may have to drink, God will help us take it.

Sometimes in answer to our prayer, God may remove the cup. At other times, He may give us the grace to drink it. When Jesus prayed "Let this cup pass," it was not removed, but an angel came to strengthen Him (Luke 22:43).

God is always ready, willing, and able to help you bear any cross you may have to bear.

"Fear thou not; for I am with thee: be not dismayed; for I am thy God: I will strengthen thee; yea, I will help thee; yea, I will uphold thee with the right hand of my righteousness" (Isa. 41:10).

"When thou passest through the waters, I will be with thee; and through the rivers, they shall not overflow thee: when thou walkest through the fire, thou shalt not be burned; neither shall the flame kindle upon thee" (Isa. 43:2).

DISCUSSION TIME

1. When we face tribulations, we are saddened and discouraged. Is this a sign that we are weak Christians? How would we encourage a friend who is going through a challenging period?

2. Is it OK for us to wish that the "cup" could pass from us? Explain your answer.

3. What biblical encouragement do we have for our periods of tribulation?

MEDITATION 31
Desperate Prayers

"And said, I cried by reason of mine affliction unto the LORD, and he heard me; out of the belly of hell cried I, and thou heardest my voice" (Jonah 2:2)

Sometimes we find ourselves in desperate situations, and we can't see our way out. Jonah found himself in "the belly of hell," that is in the belly of the fish at the bottom of the ocean. Jonah was not an evil person, but a disobedient man. God hates disobedience to His Word.

There are times when others cause our desperate situations. Sometimes we create our own "hells." At other times we may suffer because we choose to be on the Lord's side. Peter, the apostle, warns, "But let none of you suffer as a murderer, or as a thief, or as an evildoer, or as a busybody in other men's matters. Yet if any man suffer as a Christian, let him not be ashamed; but let him glorify God on this behalf" (1 Peter 4:15, 16).

Whether our troubles are caused by others or by ourselves, the good news is that God is ready to hear our prayer and deliver us. David declared, "He brought me up also out of an horrible pit, out of the miry clay, and set my feet upon a rock, and established my goings" (Ps. 40:2).

The history of Israel, especially during the time of the judges, shows the pattern of the people going into apostasy, then becoming afflicted by their enemies. They would cry unto the Lord, and He would deliver them. While God hates sin passionately, He loves the sinner even more passionately. God's grace is always greater than sin. "Where sin abounded, grace did much more abound" (Rom. 5:20). In our desperate situations, when we feel overwhelmed by sinful habits, or terrible mistakes, and we long to be free, we have the assurance that God stands ready and able to break our chains and set us free.

"The Spirit of the LORD is upon me, because he hath anointed me to preach the gospel to the poor; he hath sent me to heal the brokenhearted, to preach deliverance to the captives, and recovering of sight to the blind, to set at liberty them that are bruised, to preach the acceptable year of the LORD. (Luke 4:18, 19).

DISCUSSION TIME

1. What are some things that could cause us to be in difficult situations?

2. What is God's attitude to us when we are in trouble?

3. Will God save us even when we have sinned? What is the role of grace even when we have sinned?

MEDITATION 32
The Sinner's Prayer

"And the publican, standing afar off, would not lift up so much as his eyes unto heaven, but smote upon his breast, saying, God be merciful to me a sinner" (Luke 18:13).

Two men went to church to pray. One was a self-righteous Pharisee who boasted about his goodness. The other was a tax collector who felt horrible about his sinful life, and prayed a simple and contrite prayer: "God, be merciful to me, a sinner." Jesus declared that the tax collector's prayer was answered and God forgave his sin.

We all need to pray this prayer because we all have sinned and fallen short of God's expectations (Rom. 3:23). We have violated the commandments of God, and there is none that can claim to be righteous before God (Rom. 3:10).

"All we like sheep have gone astray; we have turned every one to his own way" (Isa. 53:6). Even what we think is righteous within us, is really nothing but filthy rags in God's estimation. "But we are all as an unclean thing, and all our righteousnesses are as filthy rags" (Isa. 64:6).

There is no one who descended from Adam, who can say that he is without sin. Sometimes it is easy to see the sins of others and ignore the sins in our own lives. We need to ask Jesus to turn the spotlight of His Spirit into the recesses of our hearts. David prayed, "Search me, O God, and know my heart: try me, and know my thoughts: and see if there be any wicked way in me; and lead me in the way everlasting" (Ps. 139:23, 24).

The Pharisees, blinded to their own sinfulness, dragged the poor adulterous woman to Jesus for His condemnation. Jesus turned the spotlight around, away from the woman, and on to the Pharisees, as He wrote their sins in the sand. One by one, as their sins were exposed, they slunk away, ashamed. What a difference it would have been if they had all come to Jesus saying, "God be merciful to us."

The cry for deliverance from sin never goes unheeded by God. There is more joy in heaven when a sinner turns to God than over many self-righteous Pharisees (Luke 15:7, 10). It sounds like celebration time in heaven when a sinner turns to the Lord. The goal of the sacrifice of Christ is realized when a person accepts that he is a sinner and cries, "God, be merciful to me a sinner." God and all of the angels in heaven, eagerly wait for each of us to pray that prayer. God will quickly cover us with the perfect, spotless robe of Christ's righteousness.

DISCUSSION TIME

1. There seems to be nothing wrong with paying tithe and doing the other things the Pharisee listed in his prayer. Why, then, was Jesus not impressed by that prayer? Where else in the Bible, was God not impressed by good deeds?

2. Why do you think Jesus preferred the prayer of the publican?

3. Write a paragraph or draw a picture depicting the celebration in heaven when a sinner is saved.

MEDITATION 33
Prayer for Healing

Is any among you afflicted? let him pray. Is any merry? let him sing psalms. Is any sick among you? let him call for the elders of the church; and let them pray over him, anointing him with oil in the name of the Lord: and the prayer of faith shall save the sick, and the Lord shall raise him up; and if he have committed sins, they shall be forgiven him. Confess your faults one to another, and pray one for another, that ye may be healed. The effectual fervent prayer of a righteous man availeth much. (James 5:13–16)

One of the consequences of sin is sickness. Every disease that afflicts the human race comes from Satan and sin. When Jesus healed the infirmed woman, He noted that it was Satan who had caused her illness (Luke 13:16). Satan and his angels are constantly creating new diseases to afflict the people of the world. Before the medical experts could find a cure for one disease, other diseases appear. But God is in the healing business. It was never His plan that sickness and disease should plague His children.

"And said, If thou wilt diligently hearken to the voice of the Lord thy God, and wilt do that which is right in his sight, and wilt give ear to his commandments, and keep all his statutes, I will put none of these diseases upon thee, which I have brought upon the Egyptians: for I am the Lord that healeth thee" (Exod. 15:26).

Wherefore it shall come to pass, if ye hearken to these judgments, and keep, and do them, that the Lord thy God shall keep unto thee the covenant and the mercy which he sware unto thy fathers: and he will love thee, and bless thee, and multiply thee: he will also bless the fruit of thy womb, and the fruit of thy land, thy corn, and thy wine, and thine oil, the increase of thy kine, and the flocks of thy sheep, in the land which he sware unto thy fathers to give thee. Thou shalt be blessed above all people: there shall not be male or female barren among you, or among your cattle. And the Lord will take away from thee all sickness, and will put none of the evil diseases of Egypt, which thou knowest, upon thee; but will lay them upon all them that hate thee" (Deut. 7:12–15)

God is ready to heal us when we get sick. David, the psalmist, recorded, "Bless the Lord, O my soul, and forget not all his benefits; who forgiveth all thine iniquities; who healeth all thy diseases" (Ps. 103:2, 3).

The apostle James advises that we should present our cases of sickness and affliction to God in prayer. We should enlist the church leaders in praying for us. God will act when such prayers are accompanied by faith (James 5:13–15).

While not every prayer for healing may be answered in the way we desire, God will give the grace to endure the affliction as He did with the apostle Paul (2 Cor. 12:7–10). The blessing may come, not in the removal of the trial, but in knowing that God is holding your hand through the trial.

What is even more comforting, is the assurance that one day, sickness and disease will be forever banished. "And there shall be no more death, neither sorrow, nor crying, neither shall there be any more pain" (Rev. 21:4).

"And the inhabitant shall not say, I am sick" (Isa. 33:24). Jesus will return and create a new earth without sickness and disease.

DISCUSSION TIME

1. How are sin, Satan, and sickness related?

2. What biblical passages tell us that God cares about our health and does not want us to be sick?

3. What should we do if there are sick ones among us?

4. What benefits can we expect if we are not healed?

MEDITATION 34
Praying in Your Storms

And when they had sent away the multitude, they took him even as he was in the ship. And there were also with him other little ships. And there arose a great storm of wind, and the waves beat into the ship, so that it was now full. And he was in the hinder part of the ship, asleep on a pillow: and they awake him, and say unto him, Master, carest thou not that we perish? And he arose, and rebuked the wind, and said unto the sea, Peace, be still. And the wind ceased, and there was a great calm. (Mark 4:36–39)

All three synoptic gospels—Matthew, Mark, and Luke—record this incident of Jesus stilling the storm. It must have made a big impression on the disciples. The normally placid Sea of Galilee would sometimes be subject to unpredictable storms. Anyone who has been in a storm or hurricane knows that it is not a pleasant experience. The disciples, who were accustomed to the sea, found themselves in a situation beyond their control. It was a "furious storm" (Matt. 8:14, NIV) that threatened to swamp their boat. The disciples feared for their lives; and in their desperation, they cried to Jesus. The Master transformed the situation from a great storm to a great calm. The disciples marveled that even the winds and the waves obeyed Him.

Sometimes in life, the storms come upon us, unexpectedly and furiously, and we are perplexed and afraid. Jesus cares about us in the calm times as well as in the stormy times. There is no need to battle alone with the storms because the Creator of the sea, and the Master of the winds, is just a prayer away. As soon as we pray to Him, He moves into action and brings calm.

We should develop a solid prayer life in times of calm, so that we may find it easy to pray in the stormy times. Prayer should not be used as an emergency device. Let's not be like the man who said, "Things were so bad, I had to pray!"

Pray always, even when things are going wonderfully.

DISCUSSION TIME

1. When the storms come, and we are afraid, Jesus cares and helps us. What assurance do we get from God's word?

2. What is the advantage of living a life of prayer even when things are going well?

3. Think of some storms you have experienced. How has Jesus calmed your storms?

MEDITATION 35
Praying for the Holy Spirit

"And I say unto you, Ask, and it shall be given you; seek, and ye shall find; knock, and it shall be opened unto you. If ye then, being evil, know how to give good gifts unto your children: how much more shall your heavenly Father give the Holy Spirit to them that ask him?" (Luke 11:9, 13).

On equal standing with the gift of His Son for our salvation, is God's gift of His Holy Spirit for our sanctification. The work of the Holy Spirit in our lives makes the work of Jesus on the cross effective. Jesus, when He was returning to heaven, assured us that we would not be left without a divine representative.

"But the Comforter, which is the Holy Ghost, whom the Father will send in my name, he shall teach you all things, and bring all things to your remembrance, whatsoever I have said unto you" (John 14:26).

Nevertheless I tell you the truth; it is expedient for you that I go away: for if I go not away, the Comforter will not come unto you; but if I depart, I will send him unto you. And when he is come, he will reprove the world of sin, and of righteousness, and of judgment: of sin, because they believe not on me; of righteousness, because I go to my Father, and ye see me no more; of judgment, because the prince of this world is judged. (John 16:7–11)

We ask God for many gifts, but one of the most important gifts we may ask for is the gift of the Holy Spirit. Jesus promised that while He had to return to His Father's side, He would send the Holy Spirit in His place. The Holy Spirit is Christ's representative; and is as much a Person as Jesus is a Person, but without human form. He is here on earth to help us in our Christian walk.

He helps us in our prayer life (Rom. 8:26, 27). He helps us develop Christian character (Gal. 5:22–24). He helps us to have victory over sin (1 Thess. 4:7, 8). He provides spiritual discernment (Acts 13:2; 15:28, 1 Cor. 2:11, 13). He helps us understand the Word of God (John 16:13). He gives us power for witnessing (Acts 1:8; 2:4, Mark 13:11).

It is impossible to live the Christian life without the help of the Holy Spirit. Before the early Christians embarked on their mission of spreading the gospel, they interceded for the gift of the Holy Spirit. "And when they had prayed, the place was shaken where they were assembled together; and they were all filled with the Holy Ghost, and they spake the word of God with boldness" (Acts 4:31).

The Holy Spirit purified, equipped and empowered them, and remarkable results followed. "For the daily baptism of the Spirit every worker should offer his petition to God" (White, *Acts of the Apostles,* 50). God is more willing to give us the gift of the Holy Spirit than parents are to give good gifts to their children. Why not ask for Him now?

DISCUSSION TIME

1. How does the Holy Spirit help us in our Christian walk?

2. How did the early Christians prepare themselves for their mission? What was the result of their preparation?

3. How often should we pray for the Holy Spirit?

MEDITATION 36
A Prayer for Understanding of God's Word

"Open thou mine eyes, that I may behold wondrous things out of thy law" (Ps. 119:18).

And, behold, two blind men sitting by the way side, when they heard that Jesus passed by, cried out, saying, Have mercy on us, O LORD, thou son of David. And the multitude rebuked them, because they should hold their peace: but they cried the more, saying, Have mercy on us, O LORD, thou son of David. And Jesus stood still, and called them, and said, What will ye that I shall do unto you? They say unto him, LORD, that our eyes may be opened. So Jesus had compassion on them, and touched their eyes: and immediately their eyes received sight, and they followed him. (Matt. 20:30–34)

It is terrible to be without physical sight. The beauty of nature, the looks on the faces of fellow human beings, the dangers in one's pathway—all are obscured from view. A person would not choose to live in the dark world of sightlessness.

In the ministry of Jesus, several blind persons begged Him for deliverance from this sad situation (Matt. 9:27–30; 20:30–34; 15:30; 21:14).

While physical blindness is a terrible burden to bear, spiritual blindness is even worse. Our enemy, Satan, deliberately inflicts some people with spiritual blindness. "In whom the god of this world hath blinded the minds of them which believe not, lest the light of the glorious gospel of Christ, who is the image of God, should shine unto them" (2 Cor. 4:4).

Even when Jesus was visibly present on earth, many persons were blinded to the recognition of His messiahship (John 12:37–40). Some are willingly ignorant of spiritual things, according to Peter. "For this they willingly are ignorant of, that by the word of God the heavens were of old, and the earth standing out of the water and in the water" (2 Peter 3:5).

Especially in these last days, when deceptions of all kinds are abundant, we need to pray for eyes to be opened. Satan will try to deceive the very elect of God (Matt. 24:24). We need the eye salve that comes from God that we may see clearly the landmines and deadly traps that Satan has set for the careless feet of the children of God.

The big danger of God's remnant people is that they are blind and do not know it. "Because thou sayest, I am rich, and increased with goods, and have need of nothing; and knowest not that thou are wretched, and miserable, and poor, and blind, and naked" (Rev. 3:17). The church is counseled by Jesus to apply the eye salve of the Holy Spirit, so that they may have good spiritual discernment.

Let our prayer be, "Open Thou mine eyes." Then like the disciples on the Emmaus Road, Jesus will help us to see clearly:

"And beginning at Moses and all the prophets, he expounded unto them in all the scriptures the things concerning himself. And they drew nigh unto the village, whither they went: and he made as though he would have gone further. But they constrained him, saying, Abide with us: for it is toward evening, and the day is far spent. And he went in to tarry with them. And it came to pass, as he sat at meat with them, he took bread, and blessed it, and brake, and gave to them. And their eyes were opened, and they knew him; and he vanished out of their sight." (Luke 24:27–31)

DISCUSSION TIME

1. Describe some of the instances when Jesus healed the blind?

2. How does spiritual blindness manifest itself?

3. What is the big danger facing the remnant church?

4. What is the recommendation of Jesus to cure our blindness?

MEDITATION 37
The Holy Spirit and Prayer

"Likewise the Spirit also helpeth our infirmities: for we know not what we should pray for as we ought: but the Spirit itself maketh intercession for us with groanings which cannot be uttered" (Rom. 8:26).

There are about 6,500 spoken languages in the world. About 2,000 of these have fewer than a thousand people who speak them. The most widely spoken language in the world is Mandarin Chinese, spoken by about 1.2 billion people! We can be reassured by the fact that the Holy Spirit can take any prayer, in any language, and translate it into the language of heaven. He can even translate prayers that we do not verbalize. Some persons have said that perhaps God speaks Hebrew because much of the Old Testament was written in Hebrew. Others have said that God probably speaks Aramaic because that is the language in which Jesus, when he was on the cross, spoke to His Father. Still others have said that God's language is perhaps Greek because the New Testament was originally written in that language. The fact is, that there is no speech or language that God does not speak and understand. Therefore, we can be confident that when we speak to God, the Holy Spirit will make sure that He understands us.

Effective prayer is Spirit directed. We do not even know what to pray for. One major reason why our prayers are not answered is that we do not pray as we ought. James says, "Ye ask, and receive not, because ye ask amiss" (James 4:3). We do not even know the language of heaven. Fortunately, the Holy Spirit can take our feeble, faulty utterances and translate them into language acceptable to God (Rom. 8:26).

Sin has corrupted our language and prevents God from responding to our prayers. "If I regard iniquity in my heart, the Lord will not hear me" (Ps. 66:18). One of the functions of the Holy Spirit is to point out sin in our lives and to help us overcome it (John 16:7–14).

The Holy Spirit is not our foe but our devoted friend. Jesus sent Him to be by our side in the battle of life. He wants to help us, but He will not force His way on us. However, when we willingly surrender to Him, He infuses us with power to do God's will. "But ye shall receive power, after that the Holy Ghost is come upon you: and ye shall be witnesses unto me both in Jerusalem, and in all Judaea, and in Samaria, and unto the uttermost part of the earth" (Acts 1:8). We will have a new vitality in our prayer life and consequently a richer walk with God.

The Holy Spirit also specializes in helping us understand the Scriptures. "Howbeit, when he, the Spirit of truth, is come, he will guide you into all truth: for he shall not speak of himself; but whatsoever he shall hear, that shall he speak: and he will shew you things to come" (John 16:13). When we understand what God has already said, we can pray according to His will, and He will hear us.

The Holy Spirit is the best teacher and interpreter of the Word of God because He inspired it (2 Tim. 3:16). Holy men of God directed by the Holy Spirit recorded the Scriptures for our benefit (2 Peter 1:21). We can trust His safe guidance when we pray for His help. We can be gratified that we have a member of the Godhead, working with us to convey to the Godhead our burdens, longings, wishes, and desires in the best possible way. When we listen to His voice we can be confident that He will not lead us astray.

DISCUSSION TIME

1. List the tasks of the Holy Spirit?

2. What part did the Holy Spirit play in the writing of the Scriptures?

3. How does the Holy Spirit help us with our prayers?

MEDITATION 38
Greet Each Morning with Prayer

"My voice shalt thou hear in the morning, O Lord; in the morning will I direct my prayer unto thee, and will look up" (Ps. 5:3).

"They are new every morning: great is thy faithfulness" (Lam. 3:23).

"Evening, and morning, and at noon, will I pray, and cry aloud: and he shall hear my voice" (Ps. 55:17).

"But I will sing of thy power; yea, I will sing aloud of thy mercy in the morning" (Ps. 59:16).

It is most fitting to begin each day with prayer since our loving, heavenly Father who "slumbers not nor sleeps" has been watching over us while we slept. "Behold, he that keepeth Israel shall neither slumber nor sleep" (Ps. 121:4). He kept our hearts beating and our lungs pumping, and He preserved us from harm. Each morning God presents us with a batch of new mercies. "It is of the Lord's mercies that we are not consumed, because his compassions fail not. They are new every morning" (Lam. 3:22, 23).

God never says, "You have had your quota of blessings for this month, so there are no more in your account." His faithfulness is immeasurable. He owes us nothing, yet He blesses us by supplying our daily needs. We owe Him everything. Why, then, should we not praise Him daily with all of our being? Sometimes we only become aware of how many blessings He has been giving us when we have lost those blessings.

We used to enjoy a song written and sung by the late Jim Reeves:

We thank Thee each morning for a new born day,
Where we may work the fields of new mown hay.
We thank Thee for the sunshine and the air that we breathe.
Oh Lord, we thank Thee.

It is noteworthy that Jesus Himself enjoyed the early morning prayer to His Father. Mark records, "And in the morning, rising up a great while before day, he went out, and departed into a solitary place, and there prayed" (Mark 1:35). Sometimes, He was so involved in communion with His Father, that He would spend the entire night in prayer (Luke 6:12).

There are advantages to starting the day with prayer. We are energized to face the day. We can solicit God's protection for the day. We can seek His guidance on the matters before us. Abraham, Jacob, Moses and Job, are a few examples of prayer warriors who enjoyed early morning prayer (Gen. 19:27; 28:18; Exod. 24:4; 34:4; Job 1:5). Perhaps we could learn something from them.

DISCUSSION TIME

1. According to the texts above, what seems to be a good way to start the day?

2. The psalmist advises a day-long pattern of praise. How can we accomplish this with our busy schedules?

3. It is a good idea to try praying and praising God all day. Can we ever match our Maker's continuous watch care? How soon do you think you would like to practice Psalm 55:17?

4. Are there some devices that occupy our attention all day? Television, music, cell phones? What are some ways we can try to "Be still?"

MEDITATION 39
The Overcomer's Prayer

And Jacob was left alone; and there wrestled a man with him until the breaking of the day. And when he saw that he prevailed not against him, he touched the hollow of his thigh; and the hollow of Jacob's thigh was out of joint, as he wrestled with him. And he said, Let me go, for the day breaketh. And he said, I will not let thee go, except thou bless me. And he said unto him, What is thy name? And he said, Jacob. And he said, Thy name shall be called no more Jacob, but Israel: for as a prince hast thou power with God and with men, and hast prevailed. (Gen. 32:24–28)

The story of Jacob's night of wrestling at Jabbok is indeed inspirational (Gen. 32:24–28). Jacob, on his way home from his uncle Laban's, realized that he was going to face his angry brother Esau. Jacob's sin of deception to wrest the birthright from Esau, now haunted him. He was greatly afraid and distressed (Gen. 32:7). He felt sure that an angry Esau would destroy him and his family. Then Jacob resorted to earnest prayer.

Jacob wrestled with God all night. At the break of day, when the Divine Being was about to leave, Jacob insisted, "I will not let thee go, except thou bless me." (Genesis 32:26). Jacob received his blessing. God changed his name from Jacob the cheater to Israel the overcomer. He also found favor in Esau's eyes beyond all expectation!

We, too, can become overcomers. God longs to bless us in unimaginable ways, but too often we let go of the arm of Omnipotence too soon. Like Jacob, we need to say, "I will not let thee go, except thou bless me." Then we will have power with God and become overcomers.

Sometimes we let go of God to cling to our idols. Sometimes we let go of God's hand to cling to our sins. Sometimes we let go of God to cling to our fears. Sometimes we let go of God to cling to our worries. At other times, we let go of God and cling to the world. "Love not the world, neither the things that are in the world" is the admonition of the apostle, John (1 John 2:15–17). Whatever we hold on to, we will eventually lose.

Let's hold on to God's hand. He will never fail us. Declare like Jacob, "I will not let thee go."

DISCUSSION TIME

1. Jacob and his brother Esau were at enmity for many years. There are some cases where we and our "brothers" are engaged in a cold war. How could we go about mending our relationships? What is the spiritual danger of holding grudges against our neighbors?

2. We cannot hold on to our vices/grudges and hold on to Jesus at the same time. Discuss.

3. What new name would you like to get?

4. What are some temptations that might cause us to let go of God's arm too soon?

MEDITATION 40
Jesus' Prayer for God to Keep Us

"And now I am no more in the world, but these are in the world, and I come to thee. Holy Father, keep through thine own name those whom thou hast given me, that they may be one, as we are" (John 17:11).

"I pray not that thou shouldest take them out of the world, but that thou shouldest keep them from the evil" (John 17:15).

"Sanctify them through thy truth: thy word is truth" (John 17:17)

It is instructive to see what the Master considered important prayer items in His last recorded prayer before His crucifixion. He implored His Father to keep His followers from the evil in the world and to sanctify them. If that prayer was needed then, it is even more needed now, when evil has multiplied a hundredfold.

Just look around the world, or listen to the news media. One will be dumbfounded by what is taking place in this world. When we pray this prayer of Jesus, we should focus on two aspects: **First**, we should pray that God's people be kept from participating in the evil of this age. The pleasures of sin beckon God's children to come and enjoy the vices, much like they did to Moses when he was in Egypt. But he chose "rather to suffer affliction with the people of God, than to enjoy the pleasure of sin for a season" (Heb. 11:24–26).

Let us pray that our church members be kept from participating in the evil around them. Our times have become like Noah's day. The Bible records, "And God saw that the wickedness of man was great in the earth, and that every imagination of the thoughts of his heart was only evil continually" (Gen. 6:5). Jesus warned that our day would be just like Noah's day. "But as the days of Noe were, so shall also the coming of the Son of man be" (Matt. 24:37). The fact is, an inhabitant of Noah's day, if he could visit one of our modern cities, would blush at the exponential increase of evil. God's people need divine protection from the enticements of this age.

Second, we need to pray that God's children be protected from and guarded against the evil forces that would try to harm them. As evil men multiply and grow bolder in their wicked designs, there are increasing assaults on God, His commandments, and His people who dare to uphold God's precepts. In some parts of the world, Christians are being brutally martyred for their faith. This will increase until the end of time. However, our prayers will form a protective hedge around God's people. Angels of God will encamp about them. "The Lord of hosts is with us; the God of Jacob is our refuge" (Ps. 46:11). Satan may do his worst; but Michael, the Archangel will stand up for His people, and we shall be protected and delivered.

DISCUSSION TIME

1. What are the main points of focus in this prayer of Jesus?

2. What are some of the attacks of evil men in the last days?

3. What assurance in God's Word should keep us from extreme panic?

4. What Bible promises would help to keep us from participating in evil?

MEDITATION 41
Prayer for Cleansing

"And, behold, there came a leper and worshipped him, saying, Lord, if thou wilt, thou canst make me clean" Matt. 8:2).

Leprosy was a most dreaded disease in the ancient East. One who was diagnosed with leprosy was condemned to a life away from regular society. He had to leave his family and friends. He was ostracized, and his only company was that of other lepers. He faced a future of deteriorating physical appearance, pain, and eventual death. If healthy persons came too near to a leper's retreat, he was obliged to warn them by yelling, "Unclean! Unclean!" It was a pitiful existence.

Leprosy was a type of sin. The prophet Isaiah describes the sad condition of the sinner: "The whole head is sick, and the whole heart faint. From the sole of the foot even unto the head there is no soundness in it; but wounds, and bruises, and putrifying sores: they have not been closed, neither bound up, neither mollified with ointment" (Isa. 1:5, 6). This is how God sees the sinner.

The plaintive cry of the leper should also be our prayer. We have all been polluted by sin. "All have sinned" (Rom. 3:23). "There is none righteous, no, not one" (Rom. 3:10). "We are all as an unclean thing, and all our righteousnesses are as filthy rags" (Isa. 64:6).

The leprosy of sin has contaminated us all. It has made us aliens and outcasts from God's kingdom (Eph. 2:12). However, through the death of Christ, we can be made clean and become sons and daughters of God (1 John 1:7–9; John 1:12). There is no need for us to remain diseased and as outcasts from the kingdom of God. For the Great Physician is ready to heal us (Matt. 1:21; Ps. 103:3).

A little fellow was repeatedly getting into mischief during the day. Repeatedly, his mother had to reprimand him. After being scolded for the tenth time, the little boy blurted out, "I guess I was just born wrong!" This is a truth expressed by the psalmist: "Behold, I was shapen in iniquity; and in sin did my mother conceive me" (Ps. 51:5). We have all come into the world in need of cleansing. We cannot cleanse ourselves, but Jesus can. We only need ask Him like the leper did; and He will quickly respond with the beautiful affirmation, "I will. Be thou clean."

DISCUSSION TIME

1. What is there about the leper that is admirable?

2. Have we the courage to admit our need of cleansing?

3. What are some of the vices of which we need to be cleansed? In the privacy of your home, list them.

4. Can you recall a Bible text that encourages the sinner who craves cleansing?

MEDITATION 42
Prayer for Unity

"And now I am no more in the world, but these are in the world, and I come to thee. Holy Father, keep through thine own name those whom thou hast given me, that they may be one, as we are." "That they all may be one; as thou, Father, art in me, and I in thee, that they also may be one in us: that the world may believe that thou hast sent me" (John 17:11, 21).

In this final recorded prayer of Jesus, His great burden is the unity of His followers: "That they may be one." When this prayer of Jesus is answered, the church will turn the world upside down. While on earth, Jesus labored to get His disciples to understand that if Christians were to unite in love, spirit, and purpose, we would move the world. When we unite under the Lordship of Christ, and by His Spirit, not even all the armies of the world can stop us.

The first disciples finally succeeded at achieving unity at Pentecost. They were all together in one place. At that time the Spirit came upon them in plentitude of power. When the church today replicates Pentecostal unity, we shall have Pentecostal power.

"Putting away all differences, all desire for the supremacy, they came close together in Christian fellowship. ... The Spirit came upon the waiting, praying disciples with a fullness that reached every heart. The Infinite One revealed Himself in power to His church. It was as if for ages this influence had been held in restraint, and now Heaven rejoiced in being able to pour out upon the church the riches of the Spirit's grace. ... Words of thanksgiving and of prophecy were heard. All heaven bent low to behold and to adore the wisdom of matchless, incomprehensible love" (White, *Acts of the Apostles,* 37, 38)

Jesus came to reconcile us to God and to each other. "He Himself is our peace" (Eph. 2:14 NKJV). Christ has broken down the middle wall. In His church we are all one. No separation on the basis of nationality, status, race, ethnicity, education, or any other criteria is permitted in the Church of Christ. The church is all one body with one Head going to the same destination.

Christ is waiting today with impatient desire for us to answer His prayer—for unity. Let there "be no divisions among you" (1 Cor. 1:10).

DISCUSSION TIME

1. Create your own definition of *unity*.

2. What were the preparations that the disciples made for the arrival of the Holy Spirit?

3. How does unity in a church or any group of persons manifest itself?

4. What are some steps you would encourage your fellow church members to take if you noticed a lack of unity?

MEDITATION 43
The Prayer of Penitence

"Have mercy upon me, O God, according to thy lovingkindness: according unto the multitude of thy tender mercies blot out my transgressions. Wash me throughly from mine iniquity, and cleanse me from my sin. For I acknowledge my transgressions: and my sin is ever before me. Against thee, thee only, have I sinned, and done this evil in thy sight" (Ps. 51:1–4).

"If we say that we have no sin, we deceive ourselves, and the truth is not in us. If we confess our sins, he is faithful and just to forgive us our sins, and to cleanse us from all unrighteousness. If we say that we have not sinned, we make him a liar, and his word is not in us" (1 John 1:8–10).

The Bible declares that sins not confessed and forsaken will only lead to disaster (Prov. 28:9). Confession, on the other hand, will bring freedom and forgiveness. Covering up of sin is futile because God sees and knows everything, no matter how secret or well hidden:

"There is no darkness, nor shadow of death, where the workers of iniquity may hide themselves" (Job 34:22).

"Yea, the darkness hideth not from thee; but the night shineth as the day: the darkness and the light are both alike to thee" (Ps. 139:12).

David sinned outrageously by committing adultery with Uriah's wife, Bathsheba, and then trying to cover it up by killing Uriah (2 Sam. 11). What was he thinking? God knew his foul deed, but He waited several months for David to confess. Only when confronted by the prophet, Nathan, did David admit to his sin. To David's credit, he did not defend his wrongdoing but made one of the most heart moving confessions found in Scripture—Psalm 51. This psalm is worthy of study. It includes many important points:

- David pleads for mercy and cleansing.

- He acknowledges his sin.

- He begs for purging, recognizing the frailty of humanity.

- He asks for the joy that comes from the assurance of sins forgiven.

- He craves a clean heart and a right spirit, realizing that without these, sin lies at the door.

- David notes that sin separates from God, and there is the risk of losing the influence of the Holy Spirit.

- He is anxious to teach others the right way.

- He does not minimize the guilt of the murder he committed.

- He comes to God, not with a lame, superficial sacrifice, but with a contrite and broken spirit.

God responded by extending His grace and mercy to David. "And David said unto Nathan, I have sinned against the LORD. And Nathan said unto David, The LORD also hath put away thy sin; thou shalt not die" (2 Sam. 12:13).

Jesus is the seed of David and will sit on the throne of David. "And, behold, thou shalt conceive in thy womb, and bring forth a son, and shalt call his name Jesus. He shall be great, and shall be called the Son of the Highest: and the Lord God shall give unto him the throne of his father David" (Luke 1:31, 32).

DISCUSSION TIME

1. Make a list of the requests David made in Psalm 51:1–4.

2. What benefits do we receive when we admit and confess our sins?

3. Discuss all angles of the sin David committed with Uriah's wife.

4. Examine the points of Psalm 51. Which one appeals to you most? Why?

MEDITATION 44
"If My People Pray"

"If my people, which are called by my name, shall humble themselves, and pray, and seek my face, and turn from their wicked ways; then will I hear from heaven, and will forgive their sin, and will heal their land" (2 Chron. 7:14).

Solomon, King of Israel, at the dedication of the magnificent temple, gave a beautiful and passionate prayer (2 Chron. 6:14–42). He acknowledged the greatness of God. Solomon reminded God of past promises; and asked for His blessings on the temple. He also prayed that whatever the need or sins of the people, if they prayed from this hallowed place, God would hear and answer.

God responded by sending fire down to consume the burnt offerings and the sacrifices (2 Chron. 7:1). The Lord appeared to King Solomon later that night and assured him that his prayer was heard. Then God added this declaration: "If my people, which are called by my name, shall humble themselves, and pray, and seek my face, and turn from their wicked ways; then will I hear from heaven, and will forgive their sin, and will heal their land" (2 Chron. 7:14).

It is God's plan to grant His blessings in answer to our prayers—blessings He would not have given, had we not asked. The need to ask keeps us close to Him and affords the opportunity for repeated contact. But God goes on to list conditions we must fulfill in order for Him to respond favorably to our requests. We must come to Him in humility because God cannot tolerate a proud, pompous sinner; but a humble person gets His attention (James 4:6, 10; Ps. 138:6, 34:18; Prov. 16:5; Isa. 66:2). We must earnestly seek Him. (Jer. 29:13; Deut. 4:29). We must turn away from all wicked and sinful behavior. God will not hear the prayer of one who refuses to confess and forsake sin (Prov. 28:9).

When we fulfill the conditions, God will honor our prayers. Nothing can be more satisfying than to know we have cleared the way for God to act on our behalf. God gets excited when we fulfill the conditions for Him to answer our prayers. That happened on the day of Pentecost, and the results were spectacular!

DISCUSSION TIME

1. What are the conditions for answered prayer?

2. What were the points in King Solomon's prayer at the dedication of the temple? How did God respond?

3. What are the advantages of the need to make our requests to God?

4. Memorize the conditions for answered prayer.

MEDITATION 45
Waiting on God

"Wait on the Lord: be of good courage, and he shall strengthen thine heart: wait, I say, on the Lord" (Ps. 27:14)

"I waited patiently for the Lord; and he inclined unto me, and heard my cry" (Ps. 40:1).

We have become accustomed to instant gratification. Fast foods, instant drinks, immediate results, characterize our lifestyle. We have also come to believe that prayer should operate in the same way. We would like to push a button called "prayer" on a machine and see the answer that we select pop out. Prayer is often not like a microwave. It is sometimes more like a slow cooker.

The great saints of God had to learn to wait patiently on God for answers to their prayers. Abraham waited for several years before his child of promise came. David did not ascend the throne of Israel immediately after his anointing. He had to wait. Our prayer should be

Teach me, Lord, to wait
Down on my knees.
Till in your own good time
You'll answer my pleas.
Teach me not to rely on what others do.
But to wait in prayer for an answer from you.
Stuart Hamblen (song)

As another song says, "God is in time, on time, every time." His timing is always perfect. The problem lies with us and our habit of hurry. When God makes us wait, it is always for our benefit. We may be waiting in prison like Joseph in Egypt; we may be anxious, not realizing that God is preparing us for a position of power and authority—something way beyond our wildest dreams!

Wait on the Lord, and you will see miracles happen in your life. "Those that wait upon the Lord, they shall inherit the earth" (Ps. 37:9). Time spent in waiting on the Lord is never wasted. It is always beneficial when we realize that our loving, heavenly Father will never withhold from His child, anything that is for his or her good.

DISCUSSION TIME

1. In Psalm 27 and Psalm 14, there are some benefits of waiting. List them.

2. Look again at today's lesson. Refer to the Bible characters who had to wait. Relate their experiences.

3. "Time spent in waiting on the Lord is never wasted." Discuss this statement.

4. Do you recall a time when you had to wait? How did the waiting benefit you?

MEDITATION 46
A Prayer of the Elderly

"Now also when I am old and greyheaded, O God, forsake me not; until I have shewed thy strength unto this generation, and thy power to every one that is to come" (Ps. 71:18).

It is a blessing to be given long life. It is the entrance of sin that has shortened the lifespan of humanity. There are some advantages of being elderly. There is an accumulation of wisdom that can be shared. There is the opportunity for mentorship that should not be bypassed. Often, there are privileges of respect and preference that the elderly enjoy. There are memories that can refresh the mind.

However, with age come liabilities. There is the baggage of a lifetime of mistakes. Then there are the infirmities that accompany old age. So many diseases and ailments descend upon a person in later life. Some of the challenges in later life may be the consequences of the mistakes of the elderly person in his or her youth. Or, they may be the result of living in a world of sin.

It is comforting and reassuring to know that God does not forsake the elderly. He loves and cares for them as He does for any other age group. We, too, should love and care for them. The Bible encourages us to love, respect and care for the elderly. God honors those who obey this command.

There are many prayers we can offer up on their behalf. We should pray for their health. This is one of their major concerns. When Jesus was here on earth, He expressed great concern for people's health. We should also pray for their soundness of mind. We lose about a gram of brain mass per year, after age twenty (that is about 20 million neurons). Just think that the average brain has 100 billion brain cells; then that does not seem to be a huge percentage of loss per year. However, the inescapable fact is that the brain deteriorates like the rest of the body! We would like our seniors to grow old with sound minds.

Let us also pray that they will remain faithful to God even in their sunset years. One of the most heart-breaking sights is that of a person who served God faithfully all his or her life, then forsakes God in his waning years. King Solomon was such an example. Fortunately, he was able to recover his spiritual connection before his death. Let's pray for the elderly among us.

DISCUSSION TIME

1. What are some of the liabilities of old age?

2. What would we like our seniors to enjoy?

3. Write a tribute to our seniors.

MEDITATION 47
A Young Person's Prayer

"And he trembling and astonished said, Lord, what wilt thou have me to do?" (Acts 9:6).

One of the most important prayers a young person may pray is one a young man named Saul, later Paul (Acts 7:58), offered on the road to Damascus, "Lord, what wilt thou have me to do?" He was on a mission of death. Misguided and mistaken, he had a vendetta against the Christians. He was religious but unchristian, and so Saul felt it was his duty to destroy Christianity. This proud, bigoted, pompous Pharisee learned that it was "hard to kick against the pricks." When Saul surrendered to the Lord Jesus, his life assumed real meaning and purpose. He who once killed the followers of Jesus, would now willingly die for Jesus!

No one, young or old, can truly be happy until he or she prays the same prayer that Saul prayed when he had his encounter with Jesus on the road to Damascus. It was a quick and frantic prayer to discover God's will. Then upon getting an answer, he was willing to allow Jesus to guide him in the direction that would bring the greatest fulfillment and highest joy. Saul, whose name was changed to Paul, became the most outstanding Christian in New Testament times. He wrote two-thirds of the New Testament books and eventually laid down his life for Christ.

As you pray this prayer seeking God's will, may God show you the real purpose for your life. God has great plans for every life. "For I know the plans I have for you," declares the Lord, "plans to prosper you and not to harm you, plans to give you hope and a future" (Jer. 29:11 NIV).

Paul never regretted his decision to commit himself to God's answer. Sometimes things were difficult. The challenges were demanding, but it was an experience of joy. In the end, Paul could say, "I have fought a good fight, I have finished my course, I have kept the faith: henceforth there is laid up for me a crown of righteousness, which the Lord, the righteous judge, shall give me at that day" (2 Tim. 4:7, 8).

God is still calling young people today to enlist in the greatest cause on earth—the salvation of lost humanity.

DISCUSSION TIME

1. What was the question Saul asked when he was knocked down on the Damascus road?

2. How can a young person tell if his/her vocational choice lines up with God's will?

3. Is the question we are studying today, a good question to ask about our social relations?

4. Search the Bible for examples of persons who operated within the will of God. Did they seem to find satisfaction and fulfillment? Discuss your answer.

MEDITATION 48
The Soul Winner's Prayer

"Pray ye therefore the LORD of the harvest, that he will send forth labourers into his harvest" (Matt. 9:38).

"Therefore said he unto them, The harvest truly is great, but the labourers are few: pray ye therefore the LORD of the harvest, that he would send forth labourers into his harvest" (Luke 10:2).

God's plan for the spread of the gospel has always been through human beings who themselves have been transformed by the power of the gospel. Sharing your faith goes hand in hand with receiving Christ as Savior (Rom. 10:9). It is of the highest importance to God that the whole world gets to hear the message of His love and saving grace:

"For this is good and acceptable in the sight God our Saviour; who will have all men to be saved, and to come unto the knowledge of the truth" (1 Tim. 2:3, 4).

God has elected that every convert becomes an ambassador for the kingdom of God (2 Cor. 5:20). The most challenging fields of souls that need the Savior are ready for reaping. The world conditions make people realize that there has to be something better. However, the reapers are few, too few for the mammoth task. Billions of people are still unwarned and unsaved! "How shall they hear without a preacher?" (Rom. 10:14).

As never before we need to pray that reapers be raised up to carry the gospel. For "this gospel of the kingdom shall be preached in all the world" (Matthew 24:14). We need to pray that the members of the church be aroused to their responsibility. Let this awareness begin with each of us. The soul that would be saved by your earnest prayer may be your own.

We must keep beseeching God for laborers to reap the harvest until the last person has had an opportunity to hear the story of Jesus. God is anxious to answer the prayer for the salvation of souls. He longs for the gospel to be carried to the whole world so that the end might come, and all of God's children could get home.

DISCUSSION TIME

1. "God's plan for the spread of the gospel has always been to use people who have themselves been transformed by the gospel's power." Discuss the significance of this statement?

2. Get together with your fellow church members and formulate a plan to evangelize the community in which your church is.

3. Remember the last time your church had an evangelistic campaign? How do you feel about the results?

MEDITATION 49
A Drowning Man's Prayer

*"But when he saw the wind boisterous, he was afraid; and beginning to sink, he cried, saying, L*ORD*, save me" (Matt. 14:30).*

Peter's cry was one of desperation. He felt powerless to help himself from the tempestuous waves that had engulfed him. Although he had been familiar with the sea in that area, he realized that he was drowning. His friends were nearby, but they could not help him. His experience as a fisherman was of no avail. Fortunately, Jesus was near. He saved Peter!

Jesus came into the world to save us from our sins. After Adam disobeyed God and ate the forbidden fruit in the Garden of Eden, the death sentence hung over the planet. It was doomed! But God, who abounds in mercy, devised a plan of salvation. "For God so loved the world, that he gave his only begotten son, that whosoever believeth in him should not perish, but have everlasting life" (John 3:16). On Calvary, Jesus paid the ultimate price so that anyone who receives Him as Savior could be saved from his sin. He is the Lamb of God, slain from the foundation of the world to take away the sin of the world.

Jesus is always near, just a prayer away. Jesus is always listening for the cry for salvation. Even when He was on the cross in pain, surrounded by a mocking, insensitive crowd, Jesus heard the cry for salvation coming from a thief being crucified beside Him. Jesus offered him the gift of salvation. There is never a soul so lost but the Savior is seeking to save. That is why Jesus came to earth (Luke 19:10).

We all deserved the sentence of death. "For all have sinned, and come short of the glory of God" (Rom. 3:23). "For the wages of sin is death; but the gift of God is eternal life through Jesus Christ our Lord" (Rom. 6:23). We were all lost, but God sent His Son to rescue us from the ocean of sin and despair. When we accept the Savior, we may join with the songwriter and sing:

I was sinking deep in sin,
Far from the peaceful shore,
Very deeply stained within,
Sinking to rise no more.
But the Master of the sea

Heard my despairing cry.
From the waters lifted me,
Now safe am I.
James Rowe

No matter how deep in sin you are, no matter how hopeless you may feel, if you cry to the Lord in sincerity He will reach out and save you.

DISCUSSION TIME

1. Tell the story of Peter as if it were happening to you. Focus on the strongest emotions you experienced.

2. Imagine you are a lifeguard. What are your first thoughts when you see someone in difficulty?

3. What role does a drowning man have to play if he is to be saved? How does this relate to the salvation that we get from Jesus?

MEDITATION 50
The Efficacy of Faith

"But without faith it is impossible to please him: for he that cometh to God must believe that he is, and that he is a rewarder of them that diligently seek him" (Heb. 11:6).

Faith is one of the most important Christian virtues. Paul noted, "And now abideth faith, hope, charity, these three" (1 Cor. 13:13). He also declared that without faith it is impossible to please God (Heb. 11:6). When we come to God in prayer, it is absolutely necessary that we come in faith.

Faith in God's existence gives us confidence that we are relating to a real Being. It is a tragedy of the worst order that many do not believe when even the devils believe. The psalmist pronounced that it is the fool who believes there is no God (Ps. 14:1).

Faith in His ability confirms our confidence that God is able to grant our requests. Nothing is too hard for Him to do for His children. "No good thing will He withhold from them that walk uprightly" (Ps. 84:11). He is a God with whom all things are possible. Unfortunately, we often limit God by our lack of faith. When Peter failed to walk on the water after Jesus invited him to, Jesus chided him, "O thou of little faith, wherefore didst thou doubt?" (Matt. 14:31). Many of our requests would not be granted if not accompanied by strong, unwavering faith. Faith is a pre-requisite to victory.

One does not suddenly possess great faith. We develop faith through practice in little things. The disciples prayed to the Lord, "increase our faith" (Luke 17:5). Day by day, we should exercise our faith in the opportunities that present themselves to us to trust God. Like other skills that have to be exercised, our faith will increase more and more.

"The just shall live by faith" (Rom. 1:17). "We walk by faith, and not by sight" (2 Cor. 5:7), is the motto of the Christian. These passages haunted Martin Luther, a German monk of the 16th century. The doctrine, "The just shall live by faith," was the catalyst that led to the Reformation. The mainstream church at that time was teaching that salvation could be earned or bought; thereby ignoring the solid teaching of Scripture that we are saved by grace through faith (Eph. 2:8). When one recognizes his sinfulness, he comes to Jesus with the prayer, "Just as I am without one plea, but that Thy blood was shed for me, and that Thou bidst me come to Thee, O Lamb of God, I come, I come" (Charlotte Elliot, Public Domain)

Then having been saved from his sins, he leaves to live a life of joyful obedience to his Savior.

DISCUSSION TIME

1. How vital is faith in the life of a Christian?
2. What are the benefits of faith to us?
3. How can our faith be developed?

MEDITATION 51
Listening to God's Voice

"Speak, LORD, for thy servant heareth" (1 Sam. 3:9).

The child Samuel was an answer to prayer. His mother Hannah was distressed that she was childless. She prayed for a child, and God answered her by giving her Samuel (1 Sam. 1:10–12, 27). Subsequently, Hannah gave birth to three more sons and two daughters. (1 Sam. 2:20–21).

Samuel's spiritual life was assuredly influenced by his godly mother; and when he moved into the parsonage to live with the high priest Eli, he continued to grow spiritually. (1 Sam. 2:26). In time, God engaged the young boy in serious conversation regarding Eli and his family.

God longs to converse with each of His children who readily listen and who will say, "Speak, Lord, your servant is listening." Our failure to hear God's voice is often due to the noise around us—the things that occupy our time, and distract us from hearing God. We live in an age of wireless gadgets. Different things may interfere with sending or receiving good signals: the location, conflicting signals, low battery power.

Our failure to hear God's voice may be the result of our preoccupation with less important issues. It may be the result of cherished sin. It may be the result of an overloaded life. The omission of the study of God's Word could be responsible for our not hearing God's voice. Sparse periods of prayer could also rob us of moments with God and hearing His voice.

God foresaw that we would be in an environment of constant distractions. He also knew that we would become so conditioned to noises, that the voice of God would become fainter and fainter. Then we would not even sense that we are not hearing God's voice. What a blessing we are being deprived of! The psalmist, David must have experienced this lack. He probably evaluated the reason why he was not hearing God nor feeling His presence—noise, too much noise. Then he shared the remedy, "Be still, and know that I am God" (Ps. 46:10). When we are still, we can listen.

We ought to remove the roadblocks and interfering signals and say, "Speak, Lord, for your servant is listening."

DISCUSSION TIME

1. Read the story in 1 Samuel 1. Imagine you are Hannah. Share your feelings of despair, pain and frustration because of your childlessness. How sympathetic are we to those who are experiencing emotional pain?

2. How do you think Hannah prepared Samuel for the time when he would have to leave home to live with Eli?

3. Are we preparing our children for the time when they will have to leave home? How?

4. What are some things that could cause us not to hear God's voice? How can we remove these roadblocks and interfering signals?

MEDITATION 52
The Last Prayer in the Bible

"Even so, come, Lord Jesus" (Rev. 22:20).

The prayer for the return of Jesus is the constant prayer of the Christian. Even in His model prayer, Jesus included, "Thy kingdom come." As the storm clouds gather on this world's horizon, we know that we must look for a better future. We will realize that glorious future when Jesus returns.

The apostle John on the lonely Isle of Patmos in the Aegean Sea received startling revelations from Jesus regarding the calamitous end time events that will culminate in the glorious return of Christ. John prayed, "Even so, come, Lord Jesus." As we witness the fulfillment of the prophecies of Daniel and Revelation, our own hearts cry out, "Even so, come, Lord Jesus."

Jesus needs to come soon to cure the diseases that are plaguing the earth and baffling the medical experts. Jesus needs to come to stop the downward spiraling of broken families. Jesus needs to come soon to take His children out of this world where demons produce more and more mega natural disasters. Jesus needs to come to put an end to man's bungling administration of the nations of the world. Jesus needs to come to eliminate the terrors that cause men's hearts to fail for fear. Jesus needs to come soon to end war and usher in His reign of peace. Let's pray, "Even so, come, Lord Jesus."

He will make all things new when He comes. He will eradicate sin and its effects on this planet. He will gather His children—past, present, and future.

For the Lord Himself will descend from heaven with a shout, with the voice of the archangel, and with the trump of God: and the dead in Christ shall rise first: then we which are alive and remain shall be caught up together with them in the clouds, to meet the Lord in the air: and so shall we ever be with the Lord. Wherefore comfort one another with these words. (1 Thess. 4:16–18)

What a glorious day that will be! "Even so, come, Lord Jesus!"

DISCUSSION TIME

1. Can you recall a recent event that made your heart long for the return of Jesus? Share it with the group.

2. What are the reasons, given in this reading, why Jesus needs to come?

3. As you ponder the necessity of Jesus' second coming, which of your painful experiences make you want Jesus to come right away? Repeat aloud 1 Thessalonians 4:16–18. Look for an opportunity to share this comforting text with someone.

We invite you to view the complete
selection of titles we publish at:

www.TEACHServices.com

Scan with your mobile
device to go directly
to our website.

Please write or email us your praises, reactions, or
thoughts about this or any other book we publish at:

11 Quartermaster Circle
Fort Oglethorpe, GA 30742

info@TEACHServices.com

TEACH Services, Inc., titles may be purchased in bulk for
educational, business, fund-raising, or sales promotional use.
For information, please e-mail:

BulkSales@TEACHServices.com

Finally, if you are interested in seeing
your own book in print, please contact us at

publishing@TEACHServices.com

We would be happy to review your manuscript for free.

www.ingramcontent.com/pod-product-compliance
Lightning Source LLC
Chambersburg PA
CBHW040316170426
43196CB00020B/2941